Comments

- **Business Manners for Success presents essential guidance even for experienced meeting planners. A must read for anyone who schedules or attends meetings on a regular basis.**

  Linda D. Brink
  Management Meeting Planner
  Leading Women Award Recipient

- **This is good information for anyone in the hospitality industry, or for anyone who simply has contact with people on a daily basis!**

  Nancy Cornthwaite
  Director, Marcum Conference Center
  & Inn
  Miami University, Oxford, Ohio

- **Marja offers great examples of teamwork, manners and respect.**

  Patricia Hakes
  Director of Human Resources
  Westin Cincinnati

- **Marja most eloquently combines the more traditional etiquette of the past with a more relaxed, multi-cultural etiquette of today, coming up with a protocol that can be used for any occasion imaginable!**

  Lieutenant Colonel Elaine F. Laub
  United States Air Force, Retired

- **After reading Business Manners for Success, I am convinced every corporation in America should include this book in their orientation programs. All employers, clients and providers will benefit from these valuable lessons in civility.**

  Patricia C. Borne, President
  CEO Resources, Inc.

D1227425

1

- I wish I'd had this kind of information when I was managing my division. I would have put it into the hands of every employee.

  Merelyn Bates-Mims
  Retired Executive, Ohio Government

- My experience as a hotel manager has allowed me a unique look into the world of business entertaining. I have seen many deals made and many lost based on something as simple as the way the host holds a dining utensil, or addresses a server or clerk. This book offers guidelines and suggestions that will allow the reader to avoid a costly faux pas.

  Gene McMenamin
  General Manager, Omni Austin Hotel

- I found "Courtesy in the Workplace" to be full of courtesy details that are invaluable in the workplace—not just a list of do's and don'ts, but readable paragraphs that really describe courteous behavior and why it is important. As a person with a disability, I was especially interested in the tips on interacting with persons of different disabilities. I found each tip to be extremely useful to those who are unsure of the way to approach a person with a disability.

  Leslie D. Turner, DBA, CMA, CFM
  Professor and Chairman
  Department of Accountancy
  Northern Kentucky University

- Marja is on target with the issues pertinent to today's business leaders; a timely guide with practical down-to-earth information with which to build successful business relationships.

  C. Michael Ellison, CEO
  Ellison Group

- As a business owner in a computerized, electronic world, I see less personalized business and social contact within my industry. Your book reminds us that proper etiquette can fade away if not continually taught and practiced.

  Henry G. Wade, President
  Wade Company
  Little Rock, Arkansas

- Civility in the workplace? Not only does Marja Barrett tell how it's done. But why it's simply good business.

  Laura Pulfer
  Author and award winning columnist

- Marja tells how to express your own unique style by investing in value, timeless line and high quality.

  Dorothy Corson, Manager
  Brooks Brothers
  Cincinnati

- In *Business Manners for Success*, author Marja Barrett simply saves your life! While we are blessed with a rich diversity of cultures and habits, very few of us know how to treat all people with the proper respect and sensitivity. So, we walk on eggs and crush most of them. This great book teaches you how to glide across those eggshells without breaking one of them. This book came to me just as I'm starting a new business. I've been saved.

  Edwin Rigaud, President
  National Underground Railroad
  Freedom Center

- Marja Barrett's etiquette program was a wonderful graduation gift for the Walsh University seniors as they commenced the journey into the world of work. The students in attendance would not leave until they each had an autographed copy of *Business Manners for Success*. This is a gift that keeps on giving...I'm sure it will be extensively referenced throughout their careers!

  Janet Howard, Executive Director
  Walsh University Leadership Institute

- **Marja Barrett's book and the evening dinner presentation were truly a blessing to our Honors Program students. Among the best students at Thomas More College, their performances in the classroom are exemplary but often their "real world" experiences are minimal. Marja's suggestions and insights into the interview process, for example, were eye-opening to them and have helped them feel more confident about how their talents can be utilized.**

> Raymond G. Hebert, Ph.D.
> *Chairperson, Department of History and*
> *International Studies and*
> *Director, James Graham Brown Honors*
> *Program Thomas More College*

- **Marja is a delight to work with and truly takes an interest in ensuring that her clients' needs are met!** *Business Manners for Success* **is a fun read and useful for both personal and professional reference. I've used it with new college graduates entering the professional world and as a resource tool with teens preparing for international travel. The multicultural sections and "Tips" scattered throughout are especially helpful.**

> Terri Creech
> *Training and Staffing Specialist*
> *International Paper*

- **I've seen the positive results of Marja's seminars with students and business leaders. As pressures of our daily routines intensify, less emphasis has been placed on behavior that adds to the quality of our lives. Marja's excellent book and seminars will, hopefully, reverse this trend.**

> Julie Boudousquie, Ph.D.
> *Past District Governor*
> *Rotary District 6740*

Business Manners for Success

Marja Wade Barrett

Design: Eberhard + Eberhard
Illustrations: Anna Socha VanMatre
Artwork: Amalia VanMatre

Published by Cincinnati Book Publishers / Jarnydyce & Jarndyce Press
www.cincybooks.com

Business Manners 2nd edition
10 Digit ISBN: 0-9772720-8-7
13 Digit ISBN: 978-0-9772720-8-2

Printed in the United States of America

Second Edition, January 2008

Dedicated to my mother

Christine Sandlin Wade

and to my wonderful family

Table of Contents

Acknowledgments   11

Foreword   14

Why Effective Social Skills are Important   15

Chapter 1   Art of Introductions   19
How to introduce people confidently—address people
correctly—when to use first names—name badges—business card
protocol—handshakes—hugs and kisses—overcome anxiety

Chapter 2   Gracious Courtesies to Observe   29
Confidence in everyday situations—how and when to extend
social courtesies—paying deference—gender no longer an issue
in business—when there are mixed signals

Chapter 3   Dress As Though You Mean Business 33
First impressions—the classic wardrobe—your unique style—
investment buying—selecting color, fit, fabric—save time and
money—where to shop—fashion and grooming taboos—dress
guidelines for all occasions

Chapter 4   The Courage to Converse   47
Connecting with customers and clients—ice breakers to establish
common ground—names build rapport—appropriate and
inappropriate topics—language— word choice—imagery in words

Chapter 5   Courtesy in the Workplace   59

Words that create harmony in the workplace—welcoming visitors—gracious office etiquette—consideration of co-workers,
customers and clients—awareness of habits—communicate to
build bridges of understanding—diversity in the workplace,
challenge of pluralism—dealing with physical differences:
The "People First" rule—family matters

Chapter 6   Telephone Professionalism   75

Answering with friendliness and efficiency—voice tone—
taking messages—placing callers on hold—transferring calls—screening
calls—returning calls—language—choosing win-win words that create
good will—six principles of word choice—inappropriate phrases and terminology—handling difficult conversations on the telephone and face to
face—reducing stress—voice mail

Chapter 7   Techno-etiquette   85

E-mail—cellular telephones—speaker telephones—facsimile

Chapter 8   Effective Meetings   89

Save time—meeting preparation—meeting behavior—
communicate effectively—making presentations—
teleconference meetings

Chapter 9   Letter Writing to Thank,   97
Acknowledge and Build Rapport

When to pen a note—how to write it—sample letters

Chapter 10   The Art of Gift Giving   109

Gift giving to build and maintain business relationships—
choice of gifts—cost of gifts—company policy—inappropriate
business gifts—gift suggestions—holiday gift giving—
returning an inappropriate gift

Chapter 11   Business Entertaining   115

When you are the host—when you are the guest—reservations—business lunch in your office—restaurant and private club entertaining—deferring to your guest—kind of food to order on a business lunch—conversation—paying the bill—Dutch treat—wine etiquette—toasts

Eat, Drink and Be Mannerly—courses in a formal meal—place settings—using utensils properly—place cards—American and European styles of using utensils—refined points of dining etiquette—awareness of dining habits—napkins—when to begin eating—breaking bread—buffet dining—problems at the table

Cocktail Parties and Receptions

Home Entertaining

Pasta Panic and Other Food Fears: How to eat difficult foods

Seating Arrangements

Chapter 12   The Art of Tipping   173

Chapter 13   Invitations   179

Extending invitations—requesting a reply—accepting invitations—uninvited guests—when you have to cancel an acceptance—forgetting an event

Chapter 14   Guidelines for International Manners and Customs to Develop a Global Perspective   189

Reduce the chance of a faux pas or unintentional offense—how to correct a misunderstanding—awareness of differences in values—business meetings—greetings—business cards—conversation—dress guidelines—dining and business entertaining—gift giving—the knowledgeable international traveler—A sampling of countries: China—France—Germany—India—Italy—Japan—Latin America—Poland—Saudi Arabia—Spain—United Kingdom and Northern Ireland

Acknowledgments

This list is long with names of associates, students, friends, and relatives who contributed or supported me in this endeavor. Since this is a book about manners, I want to thank all who inspired me, gave me your reactions to situations, shared your experiences, ideas and asked questions.

First, remembering that a picture is worth a thousand words, I want to thank my talented illustrators:
Amalia VanMatre
Anna Socha VanMatre
Mark Eberhard

Thanks to: Shawn Baker, Coral and Mark Baker, Merelyn Bates-Mims, Ph.D., Judy Becker, Wendy Bell, Sara Berger, Lisa Beringhaus, Maxine Berkman, Leon Boothe, President Emeritus, Northern Kentucky University, Patricia Borne, Jerome Bressler, Linda Brink, Mary Burns, The late Reverend Kenneth Clarke, Marsha McSpadden Clarke, Jacqueline Conner, Clovernook Center for the Blind and Visually Impaired, Nancy Cornthwaite, Miami University, Oxford, Mary Ann Courtoy, Karen Dabdoub, Council of American Islam Relations, Paul Dressell, Cincinnati Association for the Blind, Pat Dressman, Michael Ellison, Crystal Faulkner & Tom Cooney: Hosts of Business-Wise WNKU, Janice Flanagan, Linda and Hartmut Geisselbrecht, Stephen Gerdsen, Bernyce Golden, Kathryn M. Groob, Patricia Hakes, Raymond G. Hebert, Ph.D., Chairperson, History & International Studies, Thomas More College, Bev Holiday, Penny Huebsch, Susan Huff, Agnes Jansen, Betsy and Gary Jennings, John Kappas, Sue Kathman, Sara Kiefner, Melanie King, Elizabeth Kuresman, Eloise Lafferty and Kathleen Weber, Miami University Hamilton, Arun Lai, Lieutenant Colonel Elaine Laub, United States Air Force, Retired, Robert Lane, Mary and Paul Hemmer, Suzanne Parker Leist, The Reverend James Leo, Ike and Amy Matsuzaki, Margaret McGurk, Cincinnati Enquirer, Gene McMenamin, Kathie and Kinnaird McQuade, Jane Miller, Wafa Nasser, M.D., David Parker,

Kitty Pomeroy, David Stolberg, Ed Prow, Laura Pulfer, Jane Purdon, The Honorable Roxanne Qualls, Sara Repenning, Carole and Edwin Rigaud, Alice Kennelly Roberts, Cincinnati and Kentucky Post, Adalisa de Rodriguez, Bogotá, Colombia, Sylian Rodriguez, Monte and Carol Rovekamp, Jay Sadrinia, D.D.S. and Teresa Sadrinia, Lisa Sauer, Mark and Rosemary Schlachter, John Schlipp, Ph.D., Victoria Schooler, Ph.D., Marion Thompson, Sherry and Lauren Scott, Mark A. Serrianne, Debbie Simpson, Paul F. Smith, Paul Swanson, PhD., University of Cincinnati College of Business, Linda Tefend and Promark staff members, Paul A.Tenkotte, Ph.D., International Studies, Thomas More College, for his expertise in international studies, Dianna Thiel, Tawanna Thomas and the late television talk show host, Dick Vonhoene who graciously invited me to be a regular guest on his show for two years, Elizabeth Tu and E. Tu Associates, Leslie D. Turner, D.B.A., C.M.A., C.F.M., Chairman, Department of Accountancy, Northern Kentucky University, Kathleen Wade, Business Director/Teacher at Women Writing for a Change, Charles Wilfong, Mary Linn White, Carolyn Zink, Rotarian colleagues, The Very Reverend A. James Diamond and Christ Church Cathedral family. Thanks to Linda Johnson, Virginia Miles and Kirk Polking for encouraging me to write.

And what would I do without family! I thank Stanley, my enthusiastic and witty companion for his patience and suggestions; to Ann, Eric, Dawn, Ron, Debbie, Dion, Karen and Virgil. Grateful thanks for the support and love of my brothers and sisters and their families, Bob, Henry, Betty, Jim, Nancy and Nola—to my brother, John, who has supplied me with a library of antiquarian books on etiquette, manners and customs.

To my grade school and high school Girl Scout buddies Diane, Dolores, Mary Ellen and Sindy. With you, I developed a love for nature, campfires and song—where I first learned about "honor," "flag etiquette and protocol, and such things as "mother and daughter teas," and that a slice of bread is broken into fourths. To my grade school chums, Nancy and

Gretchen with whom I learned negotiating skills while trading playing cards on the playground at Bond Hill School. We were developing our win-win skills before the term became popular.

To dear friends who gave encouragement: Shirley Schooler, Julie Boudousquie, Mary Hemmer, Mary and Clyde Middleton, Alice Kennelly Roberts, and Linda Roe—to cousins Linda and Jill for keeping me in the loop of family happenings while I was writing this book.

For making *Business Manners for Success* a reality, thanks to Sue Ann Painter, whom I met at a dinner sponsored by the University of Cincinnati Law School. Sue Ann, who is a book publisher, suggested that I write a book about business etiquette. Thus, a commitment was made for Cincinnati Book Publishers to publish my book. Thanks to my agent, Anthony Brunsman, for his patience and for keeping me on a time schedule and to Barrett Brunsman for his expert editing. Finally, thanks to Eric Hanson of Emerging Technology for his computer expertise and for creating my web site MarjaBarrett.com. It's been an adventure.

Foreword

In 1986, I pioneered the first open subscription etiquette programs for business and professional people. Dubbed Executive Etiquette, it was presented at the Cincinnati Club. The press was excellent. *The Cincinnati Enquirer* covered the first session of young professional people. The Enquirer's parent company, Gannett, published the etiquette event in papers across the U.S.A. and Canada. *The Cincinnati Post* gave a full page to my children's etiquette class, which was presented in 1985 at the magnificent Hilton Netherland Plaza Hotel.

Prior to beginning my business, I was manager of the Kathleen Wellman School of Fashion and Modeling in Cincinnati for many years. During my college years, I was a professional model for high-fashion designer's trunk shows at Jenny's department store in Cincinnati and later coordinated fashion shows for Pogue's Department Store.

As an instructor of social graces at the school, it was gratifying to see students blossom with confidence and poise after only a few sessions. It was my goal then and now to offer social skills training to the business and professional people. My dear departed first husband, Bob Barrett, encouraged me to begin my consulting business years ago. I am blessed to have married again. My loving husband, Stan Harper, is patient and supportive of my endeavors.

My first clients were Procter & Gamble, Saks Fifth Avenue, the Hilton Netherland Plaza Hotel, Coca-Cola and Wright-Patterson Air Force Base protocol officers. Programs followed at University of Cincinnati, Miami, Northern Kentucky, Xavier and Wright State universities, as well as the College of Mount St. Joseph.

Why Effective Social Skills Are Important

It is not a secret that polished social skills are a key indicator of future success. We are presented with golden opportunities of relationship building every day in the workplace and at business and social gatherings. This book will help you to develop social skills that are vital in today's diverse workplace.

The most successful people are confident and comfortable with themselves, and they put others at ease by being sensitive to their needs and knowing what's expected in each situation. Thus, doors of opportunity open wider for them.

We have a tendency to think that a professional demeanor is necessary only when we are at our job. However, we represent our organizations both on and off the job in the way we speak, act and appear. For example, most social events have business connections—whether it's a dinner in someone's home, a reception to meet the new university dean, or a ribbon-cutting ceremony. Corporations are cognizant of how an individual employee's actions reflect on the reputation of the company.

Often, it's at a social gathering where you will meet a prospective client; or at the company picnic or holiday office party where a hiring or promotion decision is made. A member of management will notice an employee who is connecting with clients, customers and co-workers by graciously making introductions and engaging in conversation.

Formerly, only the CEOs fraternized with clients. Employees were not expected to entertain clients or customers. For example, accountants and bank loan officers worked at their desks all day. Clients came to them.

All of that changed in the late 1970s for several reasons. E-mail, the internet, automated teller machines and the telephone drastically cut down on the rapport-building personal time that was spent face to face with clients. Employees were told to get out from behind their desks and connect with clients and customers to get to know them on a personal level. This was accomplished by the employees meeting clients at their places of business, taking them to lunch, and inviting them to sports and social events. Relationship building took place in restaurants, private homes, and on the golf course to provide better service and increase customer loyalty. Organizations forged new ties in the community by increasing philanthropic giving, support for charitable fund-raising events and the arts.

When I was invited to give business etiquette presentations for the Wright-Patterson Air Force Base protocol officers, they didn't need me to give them training in military protocol. They wanted to improve social skills to build ties within the civilian community at off-base business and social events.

As we advance in our work and in our social lives, we can find excitement and challenge in re-examining our social and communication skills to be more effective and inclusive. Globalization shows us the need to learn and understand diversity. Just because co-workers speak English doesn't mean they share the same values. How does a manager handle diversity when working with ten people representing different nationalities? How does one handle conflict, which is bound to happen? How does one recover and move on when there is a misunderstanding?

Modern technology has also created isolation as more people are working from their homes. The challenge is to compensate for the lack of the daily face to face interaction of the workplace, where social skills, as well as management skills, are honed.

It's more vital than ever to practice good social skills and build rapport with clients and co-workers. Learning more effective social skills is like learning to play tennis or drive a car. Practice can easily be incorporated into daily activities on and off the job. And they are important in all facets of life whether one is an executive of a company, a salesperson, an entertainer, a mail clerk, or a non-profit charitable fund-raiser.

Making introductions denotes confidence and leadership.

Chapter 1

The Art of Introductions

Introductions take place in offices, on streets, in schools, at weddings, business meetings and social events. You may run into clients and co-workers during your free time with or without your family and friends. You need to be prepared for scheduled and unscheduled meetings.

Think about how you feel when you walk into a roomful of strangers. Then, someone comes up to you, extends her hand for a shake, introduces herself and introduces you to others. You immediately begin to relax and feel welcome. As a guest, it is important to know how to mingle in a crowd. Likewise, the gracious host knows how to draw in a newcomer. Good manners are about making your guests feel comfortable.

The handshake

The handshake is the accepted social courtesy when greeting. It should be firm but not a bone crusher. Grabbing the fingers of the other person can cause pain, especially if one is wearing a ring on the right hand. However, it is a turn-off to many people to receive a limp handshake. Avoid judging a person with a gentle handshake. There are many influential people who have gentle handshakes.

Make a positive impression when you shake hands by inclining your body slightly forward as you extend your hand. With a pleasant facial expression, make eye contact and listen carefully to the name. Then shake hands for two or three seconds.

Although, hugs and kisses are perfectly acceptable as greetings in some parts of the world, they are not always welcome or appropriate in business situations. Clasping another person's hand with both of yours may appear insincere on a first meeting, but is perfectly acceptable with a long time friend or relative.

How do you feel when you offer your hand to someone and it's not reciprocated? There may be a valid reason the hand is not offered, such as arthritis. A person not wishing to shake hands because of arthritis or injury, may say something like, "Forgive me for not shaking hands, I just had surgery."

Body language is extremely important when greeting someone. One should stand unless a disability prevents standing. Have good posture with arms at the side of the body and not folded across the chest. The hands should not be shoved into the pockets.

Make polished introductions

Courteous, respectful introductions set the tone of your meetings. To introduce yourself to others, say your first and last name: "Hello, I'm Nathan Palmer."

The best greeting includes repeating the other person's name when you are introduced. "Hello Carol, I'm happy to meet you," or "How do you do, Dr. Grosse." If you didn't hear the other person's name or wish to verify the pronunciation, say, "Please tell me your name again." You can then ask for the spelling. Most people will be pleased that you want to get it right. Repeating the name also helps you to remember it. "Hi" is slang and too casual for some business introductions. One can compensate for youthfulness and send a message of professionalism by using good English instead of slang.

Address people the way they wish to be addressed

We all like our names pronounced and spelled correctly. Listening carefully during an introduction will give you cues. When you are introduced to people with names like Alfred, Edward, Richard, Barbara, or Susan, do not shorten them to nicknames until you know that the nickname is preferred.

Don't assume that people are flattered by being addressed in a manner that they may deem disrespectful. It may be easier to call them "Red" and "Sweetheart" if one has difficulty remembering names; but, in the majority of cases, it is not appreciated. An executive alienated an employee who was of Native American descent. Every time they passed in the hallway, the executive would call out to him, "Hi, Chief."

Our society has become casual in addressing one another by first names with the idea of establishing rapport. However, some people are not comfortable with first name familiarity where there has not been a relationship. If you are uncertain about calling someone by the first name or a courtesy title, use the courtesy titles Mr., Mrs., Ms., Miss, or Dr. Then, it's up to the other person to say, "Please call me Susan."

Endeavor to find out how the other person wishes to be addressed. Ms. is acceptable for businesswomen, however, some married businesswomen prefer to be addressed as "Mrs." If a woman is widowed or divorced and has children, she may wish to be addressed as Mrs. rather than Ms.

A widow does not automatically drop her husband's name in introductions or correspondence. It is gracious to give both her given name and her late husband's name: "Mrs. Clarke, may I present my brother, Dr. Robert Wade? Bob, this is Marsha Clarke. Her late husband,

The Reverend Kenneth Clarke was a strong advocate for IKRON. Marsha is organizing educational programs for the children of the Windward Islands."

A good introduction conveys relevant information about each of the people introduced:

> **"Dawn, I'd like to introduce Dean Gregory, who has agreed to sponsor the golf tournament. Dean, Dawn Burkhardt is the event chairperson."**

It's helpful to indicate relationships about people you introduce. For example, when introducing a married couple and the wife has retained her family name, say, "I'd like to introduce, Lisa Sauer and her husband, Jon Moeller."

Include mutual interests such as work, hobbies, sports, music, school, travel and friends in an introduction. It will facilitate conversation. For example, "Jeff, Sylian Rodriguez is an environmental engineer."

Introductions should be warm and friendly whether they are formal or informal. Most of our introductions are informal and include words like, "I'd like to introduce…" or "May I introduce…?" The phrasing of formal introductions for banquets and receiving lines include "May I present…." and "The Honorable…."

When you introduce one person to another, say first the name of the person to whom you wish to defer. Traditionally and in social situations, deference is paid to the woman or oldest person. In the business world, deference is paid to the highest ranking or official person.

Traditionally a man is presented to a woman; say the woman's name first—with the exception of the president of any country, a king, or a dignitary of the Church.

> **"Gayle, I'd like to introduce Kris Knochelmann. Kris, Gayle Bradley is my neighbor."**

A younger person is introduced to an older person; say the older person's name first.

> **"Dean Diamond, may I introduce my niece Wendy Sanderson?"**

An unofficial person is presented to an official or higher ranking person regardless of gender. Say the official's name first.

> **"Mr. President, may I present Mr. Dennis Harrell?"**

A co-worker is introduced to a client; say the client's name first.

> **"Ms. Deborah Alexander, this is Gary Jennings, senior tax manager. Gary, Ms. Alexander is a new client."**

Even though your company president is higher ranking than a client, it is gracious to defer to your client and say your client's name first.

> **"Ms. Baker, I'd like to introduce Mary Ann Courtoy, president of The Design Consortium. Ms. Courtoy, Shawn Baker is regional sales manager for L'Oreal USA Designer Fragrances."**

When introducing a group from your organization, make introductions beginning with the highest ranking person.

When introducing a group of friends and colleagues in casual settings, begin with the person closest to you.

A single person is introduced to a group.

> **"Members of the board, I'd like to introduce to you Henry Wade, President of Wade Company." You can then introduce each board member along with job titles.**

Or, in a small casual gathering:

> **"Have you all met Jeremy Braun?" Then, you can either introduce each person or you can invite them to make their own introduction. Say, "Let's all introduce ourselves."**

When you are uncertain about how to address someone, ask. If you are introducing a co-worker, it is more courteous to say, "Tom and I work in the same office." rather than "Tom works for me."

Remembering names

If you forget a name—and who hasn't at one time or another?—it's best to be honest and say something like, "I'm so forgetful today, please introduce yourselves." If you notice that your companion has a momentary memory lapse and a glazed look in his eyes, jump in and introduce yourself.

It is a gift to remember names. The sweetest sound to our ears is our name. Some memory strategies include associating the name with a product, visualization techniques, and repeating the name.

To help you remember names:

- **Listen carefully when you are introduced and repeat the name as you shake hands, that is, "How do you do, Elizabeth Musmansky."**
  This allows the other person to clarify the pronunciation in case you didn't hear it correctly.
- **Say the name a couple of times during your conversation.**
- **Before you go to a meeting, find out who will be in attendance.**

Don't forget that you introduce yourself in other forms of communication. If you are job seeking and a prospective employer wants to reach you, answering the telephone with "Yo" just doesn't make it. Save that for your buddies.

Name badges

To help people know and remember you when you attend large gatherings and meetings, wear your name badge on the right shoulder with your name and organization in bold print for people to read easily. By wearing it on the right shoulder, the badge will be eye-level and easily read. If it is placed on the left side, it causes an awkward movement of the head when someone wants to read it because the name is forgotten or spelling or pronunciation verification is needed.

Business cards

Your business card represents you and your organization. Whether you are giving a card or receiving a card from another person, the business card should be treated respectfully. It should be crisp, clean, and easily read. Present it with the print facing the other person so that it may be read. Give your card to someone when you have a reason to follow-up. At a meeting, place it on the table in front of you while you converse.

You compliment a person when you accept his or her business card. Don't put it away immediately. Hold it and look at it as you speak to impress the name, company and position upon your memory. You can make notes of your meeting on the card when you return to your office. Include date and place you met. If a name can be pronounced more than one way, such as Raab, make a note on the card (pronounced like lab).

A business woman, who attended my business etiquette sessions at the Bankers Club in Cincinnati and had not given much thought as to how she presented her business card, said people take more time to look at her card when she presents it in a respectful manner.

Tip: It may help to know when you are a guest in someone's home that the roof serves as an introduction and you don't have to wait to be introduced. You can feel comfortable introducing yourself and mingling with all in the gathering.

In order to refine your social skills,
practice and live by them every day.
—*Lauren M. Scott, M.B.A.'04*
Miss Johnson C. Smith University 2002, 2003

Chapter 2

Gracious Courtesies to Observe

It is by our choice of words and actions that we are remembered. We should extend social courtesies to everyone and adapt them to each generation. What was correct at one time may now be obsolete or no longer relevant. A hundred years ago, it was appropriate for men to help women put on their boots for a practical reason— women wore rigid corsets that prevented them from bending over. It's interesting that as women gained freedom and abandoned such things as corsets, and began to get some air into their lungs, they were able to pull on their own boots!

Even the meanings of words change over time. For example, in a 1950s Lauren Bacall, Humphrey Bogart movie, Lauren says to Humphrey, "I saw him in Paris last week, and he was so gay." Today, the word "gay" has dual meanings and can mean "happy" or of homosexual orientation.

Kindness and consideration toward others never change. Whenever we are with another person, there is the opportunity to extend a social courtesy. Extending courtesies can be as simple as a cheerful good morning to a co-worker or holding the door for someone carrying packages. It's just as easy to make a request by saying, "Please hand me the report" as it is to say, "Gimme the report." Especially appreciated is the act of kindness such as a letter written to someone who is not anticipating it, a thank-you for a job well-done.

Gender is no longer an issue in business settings with regard to some of the social courtesies exchanged between a man and a woman. For instance, in a business setting where all associates are equal or near equal in "ranks," it is not necessary for men to wait until the women are seated. They are equal. However, in a situation where a higher ranked person is present, all associates should wait until the ranked person is seated. Today, women in business are treated the same way as men, and the only difference is who is boss, as this is the determining factor on who goes first. For example, in riding in a car, the higher ranked person always sits up front, regardless of his or her gender.

Extending a social courtesy is not to be condescending. When someone holds a door open for us, the gracious response is "Thank you." In business, whoever is in front usually opens the door and holds it. Whoever goes through a door holds the door for the person behind and doesn't let it slam in that person's face. If you are taking a client on a tour through your facility, you will, whether man or woman, lead the way, open and hold doors. If you and your companion arrive at the door together, you can say, "Here, let me get the door." Then, step ahead and open the door. The tradition of the woman always going first is more for social occasions. However, if the man steps aside so that the woman enters first, she should oblige.

At a business lunch with colleagues, people can seat themselves. However, in more formal dining situations, it's still appropriate for a man to hold the chair for a woman client unless she proceeds quickly to pull out her own chair or states, "I have it."

It is not necessary for all the men at a dinner table to rise when a woman excuses herself. The people sitting closest to a departing man or woman should pause in eating and move chairs back to allow an easy exit. The courtesy is repeated when someone returns to the table. Naturally, when one takes leave and will not return, all should rise and shake hands with the man or woman who is departing. In social settings and more formal affairs, men do offer the courtesies of holding the chair for a woman when she sits and again when she rises.

Whenever someone extends a social courtesy, it is gracious to say "Thank you." If you encounter people coming out of a restaurant, stand aside and hold the door as they exit before you attempt to enter. Elevator etiquette is similar. Wait to the side for people to exit the elevator before you enter. As the elevator stops on each floor, people in front should step out of the elevator to let others off.

Go with the flow when you get mixed signals. Sometimes, it's difficult to know what your guest expects. A television reporter covering one of my executive etiquette programs related the story about his dinner date with a friend.   After meeting her at her home, he graciously attempted to open the car door for her, but she said, "I have it." When they arrived at the restaurant, she didn't let him open the car door. Instead she said, "I have it." She maneuvered ahead of him at the restaurant door to open it and entered first. As he attempted to help her with her coat, she replied, "I have it." His gesture to hold the chair for her at the dining table was met with, "I have it."   However, when the check arrived at the end of the meal, he recalled, "She didn't say a word."

Impeccable manners combined with a classic sense of style will open doors socially and professionally.

—Sherry Scott, Marketing Consultant

Chapter 3

Dress As Though You Mean Business

Your presentation, from your personal style to the way you offer your expertise in your chosen field, is critical to building trust as well as establishing yourself as an authority in your chosen career.

It was while I was a professional model that I gained my first exposure to what goes on behind the scenes in making television commercials and the impact one can make with clothes and body language.

Representatives of a New York advertising agency called our agency on Monday to say they would be in Cincinnati on Friday of the same week to hire fifty men and women for a television commercial. The commercial entailed a crowd of people standing on the banks of the Ohio River, waving at the *Delta Queen* steamboat.

Dress As Though You Mean Business

I helped to recruit the talent for the audition and, having little experience in this area, was not aware of the selection process. We scheduled the fifty interviews throughout the day, allowing ten minutes for each interview. At 11:00 a.m. the first four people arrived for their auditions. We sent them in one at a time to be interviewed by three men and one woman from the New York agency. To my surprise, all four interviews were completed within five minutes. I said that we had scheduled interviews throughout the day. With an anxious look on their faces, the agency people told me that they had to complete all interviews within two hours and begin the shooting that afternoon. Since they were spending so little time interviewing each person, I asked them what criteria they were using in making their selection of talent. I was told, "When someone walks through that door, something says OK or not OK to us instantly. When you have a TV commercial, you have only fifteen or twenty seconds to sell a product. The person has to be visually identifiable with the product otherwise people watching will use the TV remote, go to the refrigerator, or talk with each other."

In a whirlwind of telephone calls, everyone was reached and the interviews were completed within the allotted time. The people they selected were not the most beautiful or handsome; most were not professional models. The people who walked through that door and were hired looked and acted friendly, had good posture, and were well groomed.

Yes, there is occasionally an exception. On this particular audition a bearded, portly man came in off the street in overalls and perspiration-soaked white T-shirt, saying he'd heard about the audition. He apologized for his appearance, saying he was on the job working as a surveyor that hot July day. We couldn't turn him away, and so I asked the agents to do the favor of interviewing him. "Sure," they said. He was interviewed far longer than anyone else. When he came out, he was pounding his fist into his hand, laughing and saying, "Thank you. I got the job.

I'm hired as a deck hand." We didn't have an order for a deck hand. It turned out he moonlighted as an actor in local community theater. They simply liked him and his gregarious personality and created another character for the commercial.

In another commercial—for a hospital, where we needed doctors and nurses—the people chosen were the only ones to wear white lab coats to the interview. No, they were not doctors or laboratory technicians. They simply understood the power of the visual. They looked the part—believable.

The first impression you make is more than the clothes you wear. It encompasses your body language, posture, eye-contact, and facial expression, as well as what you say and how you say it. When someone enters a room, we usually notice their overall appearance. Although, one interviewer said that she looked first at shoes.

How do you build a wardrobe that fits and flatters you to express your own unique style of dress and be ready for any occasion? Ask yourself questions. Who am I? What is my lifestyle? What do I like to wear? What image do I want to project? Keep in mind that you represent your organization in the minds of your customers and clients. An outfit you wear for a safari will not be appropriate at a financial meeting in New York. Dress one step up. Always anticipate being in a meeting with your counterpart, your boss. How does your boss dress?

People who work in finance or law wear more traditional, conservative clothes. A conservative look can be flattering without being trendy. There is more leeway in the fashion field, the arts, or entertainment for more creative or trendy dressing. Those who work in education or social services may adopt a more relaxed look. But, it all should be in good taste.

Fads are fun, but it's important to understand the difference between fad, fashion and classic styles in order to plan and organize your wardrobe.

A fad is here today and gone tomorrow. You don't want to spend big money on fads that are good for only a season. A fad may be a new color, fabric, or shape. If you just have to indulge yourself in the fad of the moment you can mix up-to-minute accessories with your classic pieces.

By selecting a few classic pieces that fit and flatter—keeping cut, color and quality in mind—you can build your own individual style. Classic styles do not go out of fashion. A beautiful sweater in wool or cashmere can be worn alone or under a suit jacket or over a cotton broadcloth shirt. Classic styles enable you to look stylish, smart and elegant; you'll save a fortune on clothes, and your career will be enhanced.

You will have years of wear from a wardrobe built on a classic look and make a good investment in yourself and your career. Since your work helps to make other things happen in your life, it just makes sense to make it a priority to invest in a quality wardrobe. Instead of buying a quantity of mediocre items, you'll save time and money if you buy the right outfit the first time.

A basic wardrobe for men and women begins with your Number One investment, which is a suit in a conservative style.

For women, the jacket should be in a basic neutral color of black, blue, gray or camel, with matching skirt and pants. By selecting a neutral color, you will always be in good taste. Neutral colors will allow for more versatility in mixing and matching pieces from different outfits. A jacket can be added to a conservatively styled dress for a classic look.

Accessories create a finished look. Accessorize your outfit with black shoes, closed heel and toe and moderate heel not more than one or two inches high. White shoes are not a good choice for business since they tend to scuff easily and distract from your overall professional image. Wear hosiery in neutral tones that blend with your outfits. Jewelry that is elegant and classic includes pearls, gold and silver earrings in geometric designs and a wrist watch. Wear no more than one ring on each hand. Add the finishing touches of a handsome briefcase or a high quality handbag.

For men, the suit coat is single-breasted in navy, beige, camel, gray, muted plaid or pin stripes. Accessorize it with a long sleeved white shirt worn over a T-shirt. Pastel colored shirts are also appropriate.

Select ties that have simple designs and small, conservative print patterns. The length of the tie should touch just the top of the belt buckle.

Shoes should be black or burgundy, lace-up and well maintained. Dark socks match slacks or shoes and cover the calf when seated. The belt matches the shoes. The only visible jewelry men should wear is a wristwatch with a dignified band and an uncomplicated face, and a ring.

Business casual for men and women does not mean sloppy. Don't wear clothes that you might wear for sports activities or to clean out the garage. For women, business casual includes classic jackets, sweater sets, pants and skirts and blouses.

For men, a blazer in navy or black can be worn with a shirt, with or without a tie. Because a blazer is structured, it conceals body flaws and creates a straighter silhouette. Khakis or corduroys for casual days are appropriate. For a dressier look, you can wear wool flannel slacks.

Fit

Proper fit is essential. It is much better to go to the next size rather than wear a garment that is skimpy looking. It is a mistake to think that wearing a smaller size will make one look thinner. Just the opposite occurs; size and appearance are more obvious.

Before buying a garment, move around in it, look in a three-way mirror, and sit in it. A garment's fit is improved when one stands with good posture. Pants or slacks should fit at the waistline. A skirt length should be knee length or longer. No matter how lovely your legs might be, skirts should be several inches longer than minis and worn with hosiery. You want to be noticed for what you accomplish and not for what you reveal.

Fabric

Natural fabrics such as wool, cotton, linen, and silk are good investments. The easy-care blends that resist wrinkling are professional and comfortable. You can perform a wrinkle test by gently squeezing a small portion of the hemline of the garment in your hand and releasing it. Check the care labels before you buy a garment. A bargain silk blouse at $19.95 may not be a bargain if it requires frequent dry cleaning.

Save time

Lay out your clothes the night before and check the condition of your garments. If you notice that a button is missing from a garment or a repair is needed, don't put the garment back in the closet until it has been fixed.

Save money

Give your garments TLC. To maintain the shape of your jackets, use shaped wooden hangars. Give shoes a day of rest in between wearing them. Give new shoes a coat of polish before wearing for added protection against scuffing.

I've heard comments from people who say, "I don't make enough money to buy expensive clothes or shoes." The good news is that you need not go into debt to look professional and be appropriately dressed. Even on a tight budget, you can find basic items that are in good taste.

There may be times when the budget is strained or non-existent. If you are just starting out, there are ways to look professional without going heavily into debt. Yes, do save your money for quality items. After all, you want to move ahead in your job. Investing in your appearance does pay off in greater confidence and self-esteem.

Since you are looking for quality and want to stretch your clothing dollar, go to the stores that specialize in clothes for professional people. Watch for sales at the end of each season. When you are in a store and you find the style and fit that you like, ask about sales.

A personal shopper or wardrobe consultant can help you coordinate a professional wardrobe. A wardrobe consultant can save you time and money. Retail stores who offer personal shoppers at no cost are Brooks Brothers and Saks Fifth Avenue (through their Fifth Avenue Club). Retail stores offer coupons and end-of-the-season sales. Regardless of your budget, you can always look well groomed.

There are other organizations that can help. Dress for Success helps women who are re-entering the workplace and have limited financial resources. Women receive free clothing and accessories for job interviews as well as counseling and training programs.

Along with good grooming, it's important to have an attractive, easy-care hair style. Sandy Rump, owner of Sableux Salon and Spa in Crestview Hills, Kentucky, recommends that you communicate with your stylist about your preferences and about your hair styling budget. Minimal is the key word for make-up. Use make-up to enhance your best features for a natural look.

Fashion and grooming taboos

Avoid ripped clothing, sweat suits, printed T-shirts, extremes of tight or baggy clothing, short shorts and cut-offs, tank tops, muscle shirts, see-through fabrics, sandals, flip flops, sleepwear, or flesh showing at the waistline, mini skirts, athletic shoes unless your job requires them, clothes better suited for evening, heavy perfume, inappropriate jewelry, teeth uncared for, body odor, bras or underwear showing, black bra worn under white blouse, no T-shirt under white shirt, slip showing through skirt slit, dirty or scruffy shoes, halter tops worn without jackets, chewing gum in public, buttons missing, wrinkled clothing, spots on clothing.

A big factor in developing a personal style is consistency in your dress. One of the comments from employers is that they hire people who look professional at the job interview. However, once the trial period is over, the new employees become lax in their appearance. In one case, an attractive woman was hired in a business sales position. The human resource director was pleased to have hired such a professional looking woman, and the new employee was doing a great job. Several weeks into her job, she came to work in a short, short leather skirt, tight sweater with revealing cleavage, and stilettos, much make-up and a fancy hairstyle. When asked about her appearance, she said, "I moonlight by jumping out of cakes at parties, and I don't have time to go home after work and change clothes."

Clothing Etiquette Questions

Q. **Is it necessary to remove caps in restaurants?**

A. Sports caps on men or women should be removed.

Q. **When can one take off a jacket?**

A. Men and women keep jackets on until the host removes his, or he invites people to remove their jackets.

Q. **Is it appropriate for a wedding guest to wear a black outfit to a wedding?**

A. Traditionally, black was not worn at weddings. Today, black may be worn; however, it's best to add color to your black outfit. I recently attended a wedding where all the bridesmaids wore black formal gowns with white sashes.

Q. **Is it permissible for a guest to wear white to a wedding?**

A. It is considerate to not compete with the bride by wearing an all-white outfit. If you wear white, accessorize with color.

Unfortunately, businesswomen are held to higher standards. I learned early on that first I had to look like I belonged to the club.
—Kathryn M. Groob, Vice President
Integrated Services Division
Corporate Marketing
Paul Hemmer Companies

Dress Guidelines for all occasions

We want to dress appropriately for our business and social events. The terminology for proper dress can be confusing, even when it is included in the invitation. Who really knows what semi-formal or business dressy means? Casual and dressy casual can take on a multitude of meanings. Guests can be perplexed about the definition of "festive attire." When extending an invitation, clarification is important. You can't be too precise.

When in doubt, ask questions. My husband, Stan, and I accepted an invitation to a fund-raising dinner for a national charitable organization, "Dress for Success." The instructions were to dress according to the black and white harlequin table theme. We rented harlequin costumes complete with hats and masks. When we arrived the night of the party, it occurred to me that we were at the wrong party. I was embarrassed when I realized that we were the only guests in harlequin costumes. Other guests were wearing elegant black and white evening clothes. However, we had fun, lots of laughs, and our photograph made the local newspaper social column.

Common sense dictates that conservative clothes be worn when the event is business related. You don't want to destroy your credibility by wearing scruffy jeans or clothing that is too revealing. Definitions can vary depending upon what is considered acceptable for the area in which you live.

When the invitation is not specific as to attire, wear your nicest business outfit. To help clarify your thinking, the following is a guideline:

Dress Guidelines

	Woman	Man
Business Attire for social events	Suit, dress or pants suit	Dark suit and tie
Black Tie	Floor length, tea length or short evening dress pants suit in dressy fabric, dressy pumps & bag	Tuxedo, studs, cufflinks white dress shirt, black tie, cummerbund or suspenders
White Tie is formal	Floor length gown	Black tailcoat, trousers, and white tie
Casual	Slacks, jeans or shorts with sports shirt, shorts sets are appropriate for pool parties	Slacks and jeans
Dressy Casual	Dress or pant suit, sweater set and slacks slacks and attractive over blouse	Sports jacket (tie not required), sweater or sports shirt with pants
Semi-formal	A more formal dress, dressy pants suit or evening ensemble	Dark suit and tie

One hour of good social conversation is like an hour of good amateur sport. It can be more than simply pleasurable, it can be hilariously amusing, especially if the participants observe good manners in every respect and there is equal give and take.

—Mortimer J. Adler, author
How to Speak, How to Listen

Chapter 4

The Courage to Converse

"I wish I had said…" "I wish I had not said…"
"I could have made a better impression if…"
"If only I'd known ahead of time who would be there…"

We've all had these thoughts. We want to feel comfortable and know how to put others at ease. How do we unlock our own unique style of conversing?

Only by being a good listener, can we respond appropriately. A good listener gives full attention to another, speaks clearly and maintains good eye contact. Conversing with another while glancing around the room to see who else is in the gathering is demeaning to the person with whom you are speaking. A good conversationalist connects by sincerely trusting and caring about people.

Establish Common Ground with Icebreakers

Conversations at business meetings and social gatherings usually begin with icebreakers. An icebreaker leads to more meaningful conversation. Openers can include comments to show that you're open to conversation, "How was your plane trip?" "This sure is a long line." Follow with a self-introduction.

Avoid asking, "What do you do?" It can make the other person feel uncomfortable if they just lost their job or have a disability that prevents them from working.

The Best Icebreaker

Mark Twain said, "I can live six weeks on a good compliment." You'll build instant rapport with a sincere compliment that is not too personal. Appropriate and safe compliments include congratulatory comments on a successful project, recent promotion or recognition, anniversary, marriage or birth of a child. Avoid compliments such as "What a beautiful dress. Where did you find it?"

Receiving compliments graciously is just as important. If you make a comment that belittles a compliment, you are essentially being uncompli-mentary and indicating that the person making the compliment does not have good judgment. If someone says, "You did a phenomenal job on that project!" Don't respond with, "Oh, anyone could have done it."   A gracious "thank you" is all that is necessary.

If you are attending a meeting, take along a cartoon, news article, or relate something of interest. It should have some relevance to the meeting or group.

A good introduction is an icebreaker when it conveys information about mutual interests or friends of the people being introduced.

Relationship building precedes business. When you are meeting at a client's office, be observant of artwork, trophies and family photographs on the desk or on the wall. By making a comment about your client's interests, you send a message that says, "I understand you. I can relate to you." For example, say, "I see by the photograph by the window that you like to play tennis."

I assisted our local Public Broadcasting Station in a fund-raising drive, and I was striking out in getting commitments. One last prospective contributor was hard to reach. He was chairman of a media conglomerate and always out of the office. I made a friend of the receptionist and asked her to help me find a time to speak with him. After what seemed like the tenth call, she said, "He'll be in this Wednesday between 3:00 p.m. and 3:30 p.m." I called on Wednesday at 3:00 p.m. and the receptionist put me through. I introduced myself to him and explained the purpose of my call. His next comment was, "I'm sorry, I'll only be in the office for twenty minutes." I replied, "I'm just down the street, I can be there in five minutes." When I arrived at his offices, I had to go through a fortress of locked doors.

I finally sat down with him after he had cleared papers off a chair. I congratulated him on receiving a prestigious award (I had read about it in the newspaper). I also knew his daughter was filming documentaries, and so I commented on that. I answered a couple of questions and left a packet of information. Our meeting lasted about ten minutes. A week later, the local PBS station received from him the largest donation of the drive—$10,000. In this case, I was persistent in getting a face to face appointment by being gracious with the receptionist and enlisting her help, and I was prepared to build a bridge by conversing about the things in which my prospective contributor was most interested. I don't remember asking for a donation.

Using Names Creates Instant Rapport

Remembering and using names in conversation creates instant rapport. When you are introduced, repeat the other person's name. At most gatherings, business and social, name badges help us to remember people while in conversation and networking.

Return the Ball

Have a response ready when someone walks up to you and says, "How have you been?" Respond with something more than OK or fine. Be able to speak a minute or two about your recent activities and then reverse the question. Ask about the other person and listen to what is said.

As a representative of your company, you can toot your horn a little by telling them your company won an award or was recognized for special achievement. We all know it is bad manners to dominate a conversation. How do we engage the person who is non-conversant? You can encourage the silent one by asking questions that begin with How, What, When and Where. Avoid questions that elicit "Yes" or "No" answers.

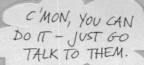

Conversation Can Evolve Easily with Self-revelation

You can encourage conversation with self-revelation instead of asking questions. No, don't show your surgical scars or battle wounds. You can say, "Let me tell you what happened on the way over here" or "I saw a great movie last night." If you wish to know something about their family, lead into it by saying something about yours first, such as, "My son decided he wants to work at the zoo this summer." This statement will invariably lead into conversation about family and you'll avoid the "yes" or "no" answer from someone who is asked, "Do you have children?"

Self-introductions encourage conversation. At a wedding, turn to the people next to you in the receiving line, introduce yourself, and say, "The bride is my cousin, aunt, uncle, friend, or co-worker." The natural response from them will be to tell you their names and their connection to the bride or groom.

Traditionally, it hasn't been acceptable to discuss business at social functions or while a guest at dinner in someone's home. However, times have changed and these are some of the best times to connect with others. It's still a good idea to be subtle. You may attend social functions where there are opportunities to network and you want to let people know what you do. And you want to know their occupations. Start by saying something about yourself. For example, if you are an accountant, you can say, "We're in the busiest time of our year." You can also share an interesting work-related incident. This now leads to work-related conversation. Wendy Bell, a fine art dealer in Dallas, Texas, inquires about her client's favorite magazines. Her client's magazine preferences give her information about the kind of art her client may prefer. Another businesswoman has great success asking her guests to tell about their most humorous work related experience.

Another way to jog the thought process is to be aware of your surroundings. Begin with what you see in front of you. Compliment the flower arrangement on the table, the painting on the wall or the view. You can then go to the neighborhood concerns, city, state, nation and world.

Here is an example of how I eased an awkward situation by being observant of my immediate surroundings. Several guests and I were the first to arrive at an evening reception where the guest of honor was late. Five of us stood in the foyer feeling ill at ease. I noticed the large portrait of a child on the wall. I asked the host if the child depicted was a relative. What followed was a story about the portrait and its history that lasted for almost ten minutes, at which time the guest of honor arrived.

A picture is worth a thousand words, especially when people don't speak the English language. I coordinated a banquet for ten Chinese business people who were meeting with local representatives. When the Chinese delegation arrived for the event at the Metropolitan Club in Covington, Kentucky, all were reserved and quiet. I threw open my arms motioning for them to turn and see the magnificent view of the Ohio River and Cincinnati skyline with Paul Brown Stadium and the Great American Ball Park. *Voila*! Smiles, chatter, and cameras began to click.

Don't get Bleeped Out

A good conversationalist is tactful and knows what topics are inappropriate. Discussions about politics and religion can get pretty heated unless you know where people stand on these matters. A dinner party can become a disaster with two strongly opinionated people. Humor that works best is a funny or an embarrassing story you tell about yourself. Making jokes at another person's expense is never appropriate and can backfire or lose you a friend. Sexist and ethnic jokes can leave you standing alone. Don't assume someone's national origin based on the appearance or name. Likewise, some people are sensitive about being asked about their nationality.

Taboo topics include personal questions about money, such as, "How much do you earn?" Asking adults their age is not appropriate unless you're filling out a business form, and it is required. Anyone present, not just the host, can change the topic of conversation if it turns to gloom and doom or a subject, such as divorce, that is sensitive or painful to others present.

Build bridges with words that all can understand. It is rude to speak in a language in the presence of those who do not speak it. Avoid jargon and terminology used within your organization or industry but will leave others who are unfamiliar with it wondering if they are on the same planet. Slang and colloquialisms can be confusing to many. A company representative happened to say to a Japanese client "Well, right off the top of my head…." The client looked at the top of the representative's head with a confused expression.

There may be times that a guest from another country is accompanied by an interpreter. Direct your conversation to your client, not the interpreter.

Speak positively about your employer, your company and the products it produces. You can quickly find yourself without a job if you're overheard putting down your employer. Be discreet in your conversation when speaking to people in public places—a restaurant, walking through a store, in the elevator, on the golf course, and in a washroom. You never know who may overhear your conversation, or whom they will tell.

A young executive described an embarrassing moment when, on the golf course, she made a negative comment about a customer. When she looked up, she realized that she was in the presence of his best friend. By the time she spoke to her supervisor, which was the next morning, to confess her lapse in judgment, he had already heard about the incident. Research shows that it takes at least twelve positive actions to overcome one negative action.

Don't Carp or Complain

Two days into the shooting of a national TV commercial, I was contacted at the modeling agency and asked to tell a woman not to return the next day. Someone overheard her complaining about a two-hour delay in filming, and that it was costing her money because she had to hire a baby-sitter. That was unfortunate because it took only two days to make the commercial. The participants received weekly royalty checks for two years, which totaled thousands of dollars.

Eliminate Speech Static

Be aware of sloppy speech habits that can mar a business person's image. Don't drop final consonants on words ending in ing, n't, and ed. For example, going, driving, speaking, didn't, wouldn't, asked, helped, granted.

We can take a tip from newscasters, who often say tongue-twisters before going on the air to "wake up the mind and the mouth." And if you are conversing a great deal or handle a multitude of calls, these exercises will relax the muscles around your mouth.

> *She sells sea shells at the seashore*
> *Peter Piper picked a peck of pickled peppers*
> *Betty Boughter bought a bit of butter*
> *How now brown cow.*

Avoid slang, speech tics such as "Yeah," "Yep," "Uh huh," "You know," "Uh," and "Er."

Try to match your speaking tempo to the other person's. For example, if you speak with someone who speaks slowly and you speak rapidly, you may have to repeat information. Keep hands and fingers away from your mouth so that you don't muffle words. A person who has difficulty hearing or who is of a different nationality will watch the lips to better understand what you are saying. People also watch lips more in noisy environments where the ability to hear accurately is diminished.

Avoid other distracting habits such as fidgeting, playing with a paper clip or pen, tapping fingers on the desk, looking at your watch or doodling while another person is speaking. A cell phone ringing while in conversation with a customer may end your conversation or make it difficult to get back on track.

Use Inclusive Words

Instead of	Say
Man or mankind	People, we, us, humanity, human beings, individuals
Chairman	Chair, Chairperson, Head (of the department)
Man a booth	To staff
Mailman	Mail carrier
Waiter, waitress	Server or Wait person

Build Strong Rapport with Word Choice

I was invited to make a presentation for the Coca-Cola sales staff at the Cincinnati regional office. As the Coca-Cola representative and I were discussing ways to make the presentation relate to the attendees, he said, "I think we'll get more 'bang' for the buck if we include staff members in the presentation." I responded, "Yes, I agree that the presentation will have more 'punch' by involving staff members." Without realizing it, I had responded to my client with language similar to his.

Listen carefully to imagery in language. Most people use visual words, *"I see what you mean," "Look at it this way," "That's an eyeful," "I have a mental image," "I'll paint a picture," " I'll see to it," "Visualize it this way."*

Some prefer and respond to auditory words (hearing), such as *"I hear you," "It sounds good," "Say that again," "That rings a bell," "What an earful."*

You may know someone who uses predominately kinesthetic words (feeling), *"He got a bang out of," "She is cool, calm, and collected," "Let me try to get a handle on it," "Hang on," "Don't pull my strings," "That breaks my heart."* We may hear someone say words that relate to food and the olfactory senses of taste and smell, such as, *"It leaves a bad taste in my mouth," "The idea smells fishy," "Let's put it on the back burner," "Let me chew on that awhile," "Last night's cold mashed potatoes."* You can think of many more.

Many of us use a combination of listening, hearing and feeling words, however, there is usually one that is predominant. You'll have stronger, more dynamic rapport in your conversation by being aware of word choice.

"What is the difference between a customer and a client?" "How does an organization refer to the people with whom they do business?" We understand that a customer buys a product. A client buys a service. However, other words are also used depending upon the organization—patrons, members, consumers, guests, patients. I had a wake-up call after completing a program for staff members at Saks Fifth Avenue. I said to Pat Huntington, then manager, that I was happy to be part of their team. She very tactfully responded with "We're happy to have you in our family, Marja." Today, I continue to feel like a family member at Saks Fifth Avenue.

Stay Tuned

You'll be a better conversationalist by keeping abreast of current events by reading newspapers, periodicals, and newsletters. Consider these as guidelines to lead you to more natural, spontaneous conversation.

Some of the most successful people keep a file on their customers and clients and review it before attending meetings. The file might include names of spouses, children, and schools and colleges they attend, pets, favorite food or beverage, anniversaries, hobbies, where they spend vacation as well as civic interests such as boards on which they serve and charitable activities.

A single word can make a difference. A manager of a credit union heard about my programs in business etiquette and invited me to submit a proposal for a six-week *customer service* related training program for the employees. My initial proposal was rejected. The manager asked me to re-work it to suit their organization. I was completely baffled as to what he wanted in training. Quickly, he said, "Here, I'll give you a book about us." I opened the book to the first page and the word *member* flashed in front my eyes. I returned to my office and with a couple of strokes on the word processor, replaced the word, *customer service training* with *member service training* throughout the proposal. When he looked at the revised proposal, he smiled and said, "This is exactly what we want." Even though every topic in the first proposal was appropriate to this group, the fact that I used the term *customer service* instead of *member service* would create such a distraction to the participants during the program that it would be like wearing a pair of red polka dot shoes with a business suit.

A person can be made to feel uncomfortable when too many questions are asked. A friend confided that she sometimes feels like she is being grilled with the rapidity and volume of questions that people throw at her on a first meeting, such as, "Where do you work?" "How many children do you have?" "What do they do?" "Are you married?" It's said that the person who asks the most questions controls. If you are asked a question, you can choose to answer it or give a tactful response. You can reverse the questioning process and say, "Tell me about yourself?"

The people with whom you work reflect your own attitude. If you are suspicious, unfriendly and condescending, you will find these unlovely traits echoed all about you. But if you are on your best behavior, you will bring out the best in the persons with whom you are going to spend most of your waking hours.

—*Beatrice Vincent*

Chapter 5

Courtesy in the Workplace

Treat everyone with respect and dignity, from the company president to the mailroom clerk. What are the social courtesies that create harmony in the workplace? How do you do that? A beginning point is to use a few words to demonstrate that you look upon your co-worker or professional colleague as a friend. How often do you acknowledge another person's efforts by saying one or more of the following phrases? "Thank you," "You did a great job," "That was really a big help," "I enjoy working with you, Paul." Personalize all your relationships by using their names in greetings and in conversation. Rabbi and spiritual teacher Marc Gafni in his book *Soul Print* refers to name as a soul print expression. Each time you use a name, you affirm a person's soul print.

Treat visitors to your office as graciously as you treat a guest in your home. Welcome visitors with a pleasant and prompt greeting. The greeter, who accepts the visitor's business card, repeats the visitor's name when calling the staff member with whom the visitor has an appointment. A guest is never announced impersonally, such as "Your two o'clock is here."

If your office is difficult to find, receive your visitor at the entrance or in the lobby of your building. If for some reason you are delayed, come out and greet your visitor and explain the situation. It is rude to keep a visitor waiting for more than five or ten minutes.

Offer to hang your client's coat, invite him to be seated and offer coffee or some other beverage. The reception area should be constantly monitored to see that magazines are straightened, debris picked up and plants watered regularly. It is better to have an artificial plant than a bedraggled plant in an office.

Show deference to visitors and to individuals of either sex who outrank you, such as senior executives or clients, customers, or your boss's peers in other organizations. You show deference when you rise to greet a visitor who comes into your workplace. Put on your suit jacket or blazer and extend your hand for a handshake. When you take your visitors on a tour of your facility, introduce them to other staff members.

To avoid distracting employees who work in open areas and wall-less office cubicles, hold meetings in a private office. It is annoying to other workers when people are speaking loudly.

Bad habits can sabotage your best efforts to gain support of co-workers and management as well as customers and suppliers. Be especially considerate of co-workers when working in open spaces by not speaking loudly on the telephone or using a speaker phone. Never call across the room to another employee. Neither should one conduct non-business personal activity such as bill paying or planning social activities during working hours.

Dipping into an overheard conversation is considered rude. An exception is if you hear a co-worker relating incorrect information, you may need to step in. To do so tactfully, say something like, "Excuse me, John. I couldn't help overhearing your comment about the shipment date. An e-mail update just came through and the delivery date is changed to June 16." If you're in someone's cubicle or office and he receives a telephone call, offer to excuse yourself.

Keep your own space neat. Food should not be eaten in cubicles. Food smells carry over into other work areas. Perfume should not be detectable. Some people have allergic reactions to fragrances. Avoid annoying habits such as filing your nails or engaging in lengthy personal calls. Turn off cellular phones so that the ringing does not disturb others in the office. Don't make cell phone calls in public places, such as the break room.

Work space and office décor should be kept neutral. If you work in an office with shoulder-high partitions, people can see what you have on your walls. You should have nothing in your office that is offensive or not in good taste.

Many people are unaware of habits that others may deem unfriendly or distant. Are you really so busy that you must walk quickly with your head down, oblivious to a co-worker who passes you in the hallway? How many seconds does it take to make eye-contact and give a warm greeting to co-workers when you arrive at work or when you pass them in the hallway? Make it a practice to begin and end your day with positive appreciative, kind words of encouragement to those with whom you work.

If you need to speak to a co-worker, say, "Tom, I need to speak with you about… It will take only five minutes. When is a good time for you?" Don't barge into his office or cubicle and start talking.

Make requests courteously and use your co-worker's name. Use such phrases as "Please," "Could you please…Jim?" "Mary, is it possible to do this within the hour? I apologize for the last-minute request," "Tony, I would greatly appreciate it if…" Do not make commands such as "I want you to do…" "Get to it right now." "Here's an order that you'll have to send now."

Asking questions such as "Why isn't it done?" or "Did you do it?" will create defensiveness. Instead use "I" words and personalize your request by using your co-worker's name. "Tim, I need that order for Mr. Lashelle placed before 2:00 pm. How's it going?" "Carol, I just took this order from Mr. Beiring, and it needs to go in immediately. Can you help me?" Don't forget to apologize if this is a last-minute request.

If you made a commitment to someone to do something and you either forgot or have other pressing duties, do not become defensive when asked about it. Defensiveness will take energy away from you. Instead of saying, "Well, it's impossible to do it all—and everybody's coming to me at once." Handle the situation with a simple apology, "I apologize, June, I'll get to it now. Thanks for reminding me."

Avoid the adversarial attitude that is implied with the words *"we"* and *"they"* when referring to co-workers of another department. For example: "They messed up," "They're so slow." "We get exasperated when 'they' expect service five minutes before the office closes." Learn to develop a spirit of *camaraderie* with all co-workers, where you understand the mission of your company and stand behind it.

When you have lunch in the company dining room, make it a point to meet and converse with co-workers from other departments. It's a good time to network and build bridges. Good table manners are just as important when eating with co-workers as they are when you dine with clients and customers. It is advantageous for you to introduce yourself to senior members of your organization when you see them on the elevator, in the company dining room and at meetings and social gatherings. Do join other employees for informal celebrations.

Conversation with co-workers should be friendly and professional. Because co-workers see one another every day, there is a tendency to be more casual in conversation.   Avoid crossing the thin line where a comment can be too personal and not appreciated, even in a kidding or humorous manner. Even though someone laughs at a comment, it does not mean it's appreciated. A man who was placed in a company as a temporary employee made comments to a woman co-worker, saying "When are we going out?" "Good morning, Beautiful." The woman laughed and smiled at his comments for six months. Then one day the agency manager who placed him in the position received a telephone call from the woman's supervisor who said, "I want him out of here now." Unbeknown to him, the woman had filed a complaint. The harassment charges were settled out of court for a large sum of money. There are many stories like this.

On the other hand, men and women should not feel they have to tip-toe around each other. Hopefully, we are moving toward a more relaxed atmosphere of mutual respect and courtesy toward one another.

Rumors should not be encouraged. They can come back to haunt you if you listen or participate in conversations that are gossipy. If someone asks you, "Did you hear about the affair so and so is having with…?" respond with, "Oh, I don't pay attention to gossip"—and change the subject.

Look like you're ready for business every day, even on casual dress days. You want to look professional especially if you are meeting customers and clients. Follow the dress guidelines of your company and don't skirt around them.

Your company restroom should be just as clean as the reception area. It is inconsiderate to leave a sloppy washbowl for the next person whether it is your own company's restroom or a public facility. After washing the hands, it takes just a few seconds to tidy-up the counter with a paper towel.

Opportunities for employees to work from home are increasing. If you are a telecommuter and have the good fortune of working from home, don't pretend that you're working when you're not.

I thank my staff at the end of the day for their help with the patients that day.
—Wafa Nasser, M.D.

Respect, uphold and support your company's ethics policies by your actions. Everyone, from the mail clerk to the president, is a role model for courteous and considerate behavior.

Diversity in the Workplace
The challenge of pluralism

To work effectively with others, one needs to understand and work with all the factors that exist in today's workplace: cultural backgrounds and values, physical abilities and disabilities that are temporary or permanent, gender, religion, personalities, and diversity of working styles based on personality types.

How does a manager in a multinational company handle the diversity when meeting with ten people representing Japan, China, Malaysia, and the Hispanic and African-American cultures? How do you behave with respect toward people of other cultures? How do you take control of the situation and move on when there has been a breakdown in communication?

To foster a respectful attitude and work more harmoniously:

1. Develop a global mentality. Be willing to work with people across cultures.
2. Do not be judgmental.
3. Be yourself.
4. Be aware that there are differences; that you can't avoid conflict; there will be miscommunications.
5. Realize that none of us is perfect.
6 Be willing to apologize.

An apology opens up the door to review a mistake and resolve a conflict in an acceptable way. Apologizing has nothing to do with who made the mistake. By preparing yourself, you'll be able to get out of difficult situations. Say, "I'm sorry" or "I apologize, let's begin again. What do you need to know?"

Practical jokes are not always understood by people of other cultures and can backfire. Say, "I'm sorry. In our society, this kind of humor is acceptable."

The interpretation of body language is often not accurate. For example: African American children frequently do not look into the faces of adults. They will drop their heads when speaking with you. It is a habit that has come down through generations as a sign of respect to adults. This habit may continue into adulthood. It does not denote untrustworthiness or a lack of respect.

Dealing with Physical Differences
'People first rule'

The "people first" rule says that we are people first and only secondarily people who have disabilities. Do not identify the whole person by a disability, that is, "Judy is a paraplegic." Instead say "Judy is someone who has paraplegia." People are not wheelchair bound or confined to a wheelchair. They use wheelchairs.

When conversing with someone who uses a wheelchair or scooter, pull up a chair and sit so that you are at a comfortable eye-level. Do not stand over him to converse since it puts a strain on the neck to look up for any length of time. Do not kneel to greet or converse with someone who uses a wheelchair or scooter, as it may appear condescending. Never push someone's wheelchair without permission. Some people who use wheelchairs do not want assistance; others welcome it. If a person who uses a scooter transfers to a regular seat, do not sit on the unoccupied scooter or hang coats on it. A friend who uses a scooter says, "I like it when people open doors or "run interference" through a crowd for me. I like it if someone asks if they can bring me a drink or help me fill a plate at a buffet. I think it is really nice if they ask if someone else is helping me and, if not, then offering to help."

If you are at a social gathering, offer to bring food or a beverage for the person in a wheelchair.

One of the questions I have been asked is how to shake hands with someone who has lost his right hand. When you shake hands with someone who has lost the right hand, treat the person just as you would any other person. If the arm is extended to you, reach out and touch it. When a person's hand is disfigured by arthritis or an accident, touch it lightly.

Face the person with a hearing impairment and speak distinctly and slowly using your lips to form the words. Don't turn your head to the side or put your hands over your mouth as you speak. The person who is hearing impaired is reading your lips and facial expression. As an exercise to sensitize you to the challenges of hearing impairment and to speak more distinctly yourself, watch TV news anchors, but turn off the sound. See if you can understand what is being said by watching lips and facial expressions.

You will startle a person with visual impairment, just as you would anyone, if you grab the arm in an attempt to assist. Face the person and introduce yourself. Ask first if the individual wants assistance. Don't be afraid to ask for guidance in order to assist properly.

A sight-impaired individual may use a cane or have a guide dog. The inclination for most of us is to reach down and pet the dog. Be respectful of the fact that a guide dog has a job to do and shouldn't be distracted. Do not call out to the dog—or pet it—without permission.

Visually impaired people work successfully with adaptive technologies that include using a large font or a combination of large font and speech, or speech by itself and Braille.

People with visual impairments are often compensated with other highly developed senses and acquire alternate techniques, not so much miraculous as evolutionary. For example, even though a person is sightless, there is sensitivity to knowing when someone is really paying attention and making eye-contact while conversing, just as much as a sighted person.

A great opportunity awaits family businesses that can separate responsibility and decision-making from family expectations.
—Paul Hemmer, President
Hemmer Companies

Family Business Matters

There are many advantages to being part of a family-owned organization such as trust in one another, familiarity, heightened communication and shared values, which enables rapid growth of the organization.

In a family run business, professional boundaries need to be maintained. People who are outside the family will notice any family clique, and so a son or daughter working in the business should not expect preferred treatment. Non-family members will notice and resent that it is only the siblings who get the new computers or laptops. Children and siblings in business don't critique or become emotional in a business meeting. The wise son or daughter, with an eye on long term success, learns to listen to others objectively, but not be used as a wedge by employees who want to resolve issues. Parents can help their children with this skill by teaching them to think and act independently in responsible ways.

In addition, family members working together day-in and day-out need to remember not to take each other for granted, but to treat each other as they would another professional.

People who have run family owned businesses recommend that children work other places before joining the family business. Decisions to hire family members should be considered carefully and not made during the holidays when spirits are high.

As a family member in the organization, you represent yourself, your family, and your organization both on and off the job. When you read in the newspaper about someone who has broken the law or acted unethically, the occupation, organization and family ties are always mentioned. Family members are held to a higher set of standards within an organization. Family members should respect the family into which they are born or marry. They have the opportunity to enhance the family name.

Trust-building with customers can be powerful when there is a family relationship. The trust-building is initiated at the first meeting. More and more bright, capable women are inheriting their father's place as presidents of their companies. In my research for this book, one story stands out. Karen attended sales meetings with her father who was the president of a large printing company. Karen was reluctant to be open about the family relationship at meetings with customers. In her effort to seem independent; that she didn't get the job because she was the president's daughter, she introduced herself as the new account manager without the father-daughter reference. The lack of forthrightness backfired. After several meetings, the customer learned about the relationship from a third party. The customer was surprised that their father-daughter relationship was not disclosed in the initial introduction, and disappointed that they had not been honest about the relationship. The customer also thought they did not trust him to do business with the daughter if he learned about the relationship.

Most family run businesses do not survive through the second generation. Relatives are known to have spats. Not every family disagreement has an immediate resolution. Know how to begin again and be sincere in your wish to improve your relationship. If there is a choice of resolution, it will begin with sincerity. Don't close the door as Joan wished to do. Joan, a sibling, had an on-going personality conflict with her brother and at times she wanted to sever all ties with him. In her heart, she knew he was there for her if there was a crisis. So, Joan improved her communication skills and became a better listener. She and her brother are now much closer and have a good business relationship. The change in their relationship had a ripple effect and their relationship with the other siblings improved as well. Positive moments are collective resulting in a positive relationship.

The supportive spouse

Spouses have a special role to play in being supportive of one another. When both have demanding careers and family obligations, conflicting priorities can arise. For example, it may not always be possible to attend business and social functions together.

When you both attend an event, prepare your partner. If your partner is comfortable at an event, you'll have a more enjoyable and successful time. Give your spouse as much information as possible about the purpose of the event, names and job titles of people who are invited, with whom you will be seated at dinner and the proper attire. If necessary, make telephone calls to the event planner or host to get information.

Unless you are in a receiving line, spouses should circulate separately among their guests. If you stay with your spouse all evening, people will not get to know you as an individual. Be willing to go beyond your comfort zone. Conversation, when together, does not cross the line into inappropriateness such as jokes or comments that can backfire. You may call your spouse "Love Flower" at home, but not at her business function.

Actions of the spouse can have a positive or negative effect. A lovely friend, I'll refer to as Carol, whose husband, Fred, is a corporate president of a large construction company, refers to her role as a supportive spouse. And what a great support she is. Carol had a vibrant career when she met and married her husband who was in a competing business. He jokingly says he had to marry her to get her away from the competition. They now have small children. Carol and Fred are leaders in the community and they support and promote many philanthropic causes. She says that when attending or hosting business events, "You're there to greet and converse and do all you can to make your partner look good." Being the spouse of the president, Carol observes boundaries. She and their children never ask personal favors of Fred's secretary. Although people constantly seek her advice, she does not involve herself in intricate business discussions if it's not her business. Nor does she feel like she has to answer every question or share opinions about her spouse's business matters. Carol says "Loose lips can undermine other people's hard working efforts by passing on proprietary information that is shared with you." Occasionally, at a social function, someone will ask Carol for some inside information about the business. Her gentle, tactful response is, "You'll have to get with Fred on that." When information is shared with you, it's important to use good judgment and not repeat information at a weak moment.

Fred's siblings also work in the business and their families gather for holiday celebrations. Because of Fred's position, he has the monetary compensation that allows him, Carol and their children to travel. In addition, their prominence in the community includes recognition and attendance at high level business and social functions. Because of the disparity in their lifestyle and the lifestyles of other family members, Carol is careful to be discreet at family gatherings. She tones down her dress when she is with her sister-in-laws. She doesn't wear high fashion or skin tight clothes, or brag about the dinners they attend. And Fred understands that when they are at a nephew's graduation party, that is not the time to sit down and work out a business deal.

The Stay-at-Home Spouse

Some couples make the choice that one will stay at home and be a nurturing spouse, and it can be the husband or wife who nurtures a partner's career. Such an arrangement is a special relationship of empowerment rather than a financial partnership. The division of financial resources is not fifty-fifty. The partner who stays home with their young children finds other ways to support by taking an active role in the community, volunteering at their children's school or involvement in other philanthropic endeavors. There are some successful partnerships that reverse the stay-at-home nurturing role after a few years to enable a partner to return to school or pursue a career.

Surely whoever speaks to me in the right voice, him or her I shall follow.

— Walt Whitman

Chapter 6

Telephone Professionalism Welcomes Business

The telephone is the front door to your organization. You create business or lose business every time the telephone is answered. Each time you answer the telephone you send a message about you and your company. Credibility is diminished if calls are answered with an uncaring attitude. Whoever answers a telephone call must take ownership by seeing that it is handled efficiently. This means transferring to the right person, taking messages and any other follow-up that may be required. The person on the other end is not an interruption. The person on the other end is the reason for your business.

When we are face to face with someone, it's easier to build rapport and make a positive first impression. We can make eye contact, shake hands, and see the facial expression. We can observe their work environment, pictures and other memorabilia on their desk, all of which helps us find common ground for conversation. But, on the telephone, we have only our voice to convey a message of friendliness, efficiency, trust and caring. It takes only an instant for someone to decide if they want to do business with us or not, based just on hearing our voice.

In addition, one's body language communicates subtle and obvious impressions to the caller. If the posture is good, the tone of voice will be confident. Good posture reduces stress because the lungs are able to take in more oxygen. Correct breathing gives the voice more energy. If one slumps, the voice will sound lethargic. Rolling the eyes in a "here we go again" attitude can create an impatient tone of voice. Distractions such as continuing to read or browsing the internet while you are speaking with another will also communicate a disinterested tone of voice.

Considerate communication should encompass everyone. Treat internal calls as professionally as calls with clients and customers. Since employees in a company are inter-dependent, it's important to build bridges with those with whom we work closest—our co-workers and those from other departments. If a co-worker calls with a request, it's rude to say, "I'm too busy to get it for you right now." A better response is "Josh, I'll be happy to send you a copy. When do you need it?" If you are in the middle of a critical project, you can explain that to your co-worker and, together, agree upon a time when you are able to help Josh.

Neither should one stand in front of the desk or in the doorway waiting for another person to hang up the telephone. If you see that someone is speaking on the telephone, leave and come back later. If you have a visitor in your office and you are summoned to take a personal or confidential call, excuse yourself and take the call in another location, allowing your visitor to remain seated.

The telephone should be answered within the first three rings. Speak in a warm, but professional tone of voice. Give the caller your undivided attention.

Sample Answers

"Good morning, Whole Child Pediatric."

"Thank you for calling BeeDazzled Gardens and Design. This is Dawn Hummel. How may I help you?"

If you are answering your department's telephone, give your name and department.

"Becky Wade, accounting department."

If you must place someone on hold, be courteous and ask permission, "Would you please hold the line?" or "Are you able to hold?" Wait for the caller to give permission or if there is no response (remember, you can't see them and they may be shaking their head up and down), thank the caller for holding and then place them on hold. Don't place a caller on hold for more than thirty seconds. If there is a longer wait, offer to take a message. You can also offer to transfer the caller to a voice mailbox.

When transferring a call, explain the reason for the transfer. "I'm going to transfer you to Thomas Day, who has that information. Please hold the line while I transfer your call." It's a good idea to give the extension number of the person to whom the call is being transferred. Say, "For your information, that extension number is . . ." Don't say, "Just in case you get cut off, here is the extension number."

To save time, work toward reducing the number of calls transferred. According to an article in the *Wall Street Journal*, statistics show that fifty percent of calls would not have to be returned if the staff person answering a call were to reintroduce himself and offer to help. In other words, there may be someone in the office who has the information that the caller needs.

> **"Bud Roe is out of the office today. This is Pat Wesdorp. May I help you?"**

If you need to transfer an angry caller, inform your co-worker before you transfer the call.

People don't mind if you screen their calls if it's done correctly. It's offensive to say "Who's calling?" Instead say, "May I tell her who is calling." Since you have asked the name of the caller, it is courteous for the person who is called to address the caller by name when she picks up the telephone so that the caller doesn't have to repeat it.

You can save time and avoid the screening process when you place calls if you identify yourself and your organization immediately. For example, "Hello, this is Donna Salyers from Fabulous Furs, may I speak with Linda Roe?"

Always treat a message-taker respectfully and always ask the name of the message-taker. If you befriend a message-taker, he'll probably be able to tell you the best time to reach the person you are calling.

If you leave a message that you will call back at a specific date and time, you have made a telephone appointment that is just as binding as a face to face appointment. Mark it on your calendar so that you don't forget it.

Assure that your message is delivered by thanking the message-taker by name.

> **"Thank you, Tony, for taking this message and giving it to Shelly Riddle."**

If you are the message-taker for someone else, write out a complete message and verify the correct spelling of the name and company name; record the day, date, and time as well as your name or initials.

Returning calls promptly is another way to demonstrate the efficiency and dependability of your organization. When you return a call, make it easy for the message-taker by identifying yourself and your organization. You will expedite your call if you give a reason. "This is Jane Miller returning Ms. Beers' call."

People remember most what you say last. If it is necessary to interrupt or terminate a call, do so politely. Make your last words positive, helpful and hopeful. Review your conversation and what action you are going to take. Provide assurance that you will fulfill any promises, and end by letting the caller know that you are available for future assistance. Thank the caller.

The general rule is that whoever places the call is the last one to hang up. It also gives the person called a chance to add something.

Sometimes an angry caller may catch you off guard. It's important to understand that the anger is not directed at you personally. For example, if a caller says, "I'm calling about an incorrect bill you sent me." Don't waste time thinking about whose fault it is. Don't say, "I didn't send you a bill." Neither should you pass the buck by saying, "That bill was sent by the accounting department." Instead, think about what you can do as a next step to help the caller. You have an opportunity to turn the situation into a positive one for you, your organization and the caller.

There are times when an apology is needed. It's all right to apologize for an error or an inconvenience even though it was not your fault. If a caller is upset that a caterer did not arrive on time, it is appropriate and necessary to show that you care. Empathize by saying with sincerity, "I apologize for this inconvenience." Then, follow with what you are going to do to satisfy the client.

You'll convey a willingness to help if you maintain your composure and listen to the caller. You can calm an emotional person by using her name in conversation. Using the name reassures the caller that she will receive personal attention. Your conversation should reflect a positive tone with reassurance that the caller will be helped in a prompt and satisfying manner.

You can communicate more effectively when you are aware of your word choice. The right words can reassure, inspire, motivate and build trust. They can calm an angry customer, parent or child, or diffuse a difficult situation. Inappropriate language can annoy, offend, create roadblocks and defensiveness. Choose words that create good-will and rapport. Greater cooperation is gained by what you say and how you say it.

Here are six basic principles to guide you in positive word choice.

1. **Frame responses positively.** "I'll be happy to check that for you." "I'll be glad to help you."

2. **Use collaborative language.** "Let's see how we can correct this. We appreciate it when customers bring such matters to our attention. It helps us to give better service."

3. **Avoid words that suggest customer error.** Saying, "Why didn't you . . .?" creates defensiveness. Don't waste time thinking about who is right and who is wrong. You can still be an advocate to the client in finding a solution.

4. **Avoid using the words "problem" and "complaint."** These words escalate emotion in a difficult situation. Instead, say, "What is your concern?" "We'll be happy to correct this situation."

5. **Be specific about follow-up** to assure your client of your care and attention to the matter.

6. **Make requests courteously.** Do not make commands, such as "You'll have to." Instead say, "Please call Mary about . . ." or "Please sign the form and return it to . . ."

Below are ten inappropriate phrases and their more courteous response. As you read each one, think about the above principle to which it corresponds.

"There's nothing I can do." Instead say, "How can I help you?" Or "I'll find someone who can help you."

"I disagree." Saying these words will create a roadblock. Instead of disagreeing, seek to understand. Say, "I understand and . . ." You can then state your thoughts or solution.

"Do you understand?" Use "I" instead of "you." "Is there anything more I can tell you?" "I'll be happy to go over it with you."

"I'll try" is weak. It means maybe you will, and maybe you won't. Be reassuring with "I will."

"What's your problem?" Instead say, "How can I help you?" "Please tell me your concern." "What is your question?" "Please explain the situation."

"I can't" should be "I will" (help you).

"That's not my job" is never appropriate. Instead say, "I'll be happy to help you."

"I see what you're saying, *but* . . ." Saying "but" throws up a roadblock. Say, "I see what you're saying <u>and</u> . . ."

"It's company policy." Don't hide behind rules and company policy when denying a customer's request. In the client's mind, it's all about him and his satisfaction.

Saying "Why didn't you . . .?" creates defensiveness.

If for some reason you have to say "No," try to set up conditions where you can fulfill the request.

Stressful situations can take their physical toll on your health. If you are on the telephone frequently, wear a comfortable headset so that you don't incur back and neck strain.

Maintain good posture so that you can breathe from the diaphragm. Your voice will sound more alive by doing so, and you'll feel better throughout the day.

Sip water throughout the day. Stand occasionally as you speak to relieve monotony and improve your circulation. Go outside for a breath of fresh air on your breaks and at lunch time.

Voice Mail

When leaving a voice mail message, clearly state your name, organization, and telephone number and the reason for your call. It's a good idea to state your telephone number twice. A garbled message will not elicit a return call. Do not leave a confidential message on voice mail. Instead, ask for a return call.

Voice mail dumping is annoying. If you are making the overture or solicitation call, don't ask the person you are soliciting to return your call. Do leave a message, but add, "There's no need to call me back. I'll follow-up."

Update your voice mail daily. Inform callers when you will be in the office and when you can return the call. Give a referral name and number in case the caller needs immediate assistance. Call back within twenty-four hours.

Tip: **A businesswoman leaves me voice mail messages. She always ends with a friendly, sincere sounding, "Marja, I look forward to speaking with you." Guess whose message I return first?**

Chapter 7

Techno-etiquette

E-mail messages—because of their ease, speed and simplicity—are less formal, but they should always be polite. Each e-mail message is a reflection of you and your organization.

E-mail messages are used for brief messages to confirm appointments and to acknowledge information received via e-mail. They are not intended for substantive information when a letter would be better.

Care should always be taken to make sure that spelling and grammar are correct. Use spell check, but don't depend entirely on it. A word may not be caught by spell check that can otherwise change the entire meaning of your message. Enlist the help of a trusted co-worker to look over your correspondence.

The tone of the e-mail letter should always be polite. Something said face to face in a joking manner may not come across the same way in your e- mail message. You'll be less apt to be abrupt if you read your message aloud before sending it. Sensitive issues should be handled face to face.

Never "flame" by saying anything in anger or outrage, such as: "How can he be such an idiot?"

E-mail messages are not always private, and a systems glitch can misdirect e-mail messages.   You usually can't retrieve a message once you hit the send button. In addition, computers and their hard drives belong to the company which makes it permissible to investigate employees' hard drives.

If your message is of a confidential nature, use the telephone instead of e-mail.

Don't send e-mail messages that will interfere with another person's work, such as long personal missives, chain letters or spam.

Some people do not like their e-mail address distributed indiscriminately. Use discretion when sending out a mass electronic mailing.

Just as you would in a telephone or face to face conversation, avoid unusual abbreviations and acronyms. The recipient may not be familiar with them. Beginning sentences and names with lower case letters is annoying to the reader and detracts from your letter. You don't want to convey a message of sloppiness or that you were so hurried that you couldn't communicate properly.

Avoid substandard English and slang in your e-mails. Using all capitals implies shouting.

To close friends, emoticons may be used sparingly to communicate feelings such as (:) parenthesis and colon to denote happy or (: (to denote sadness. Omit them for your professional correspondence. You want to be taken seriously.

Speaker telephones

A speaker telephone should never be used without the permission of the caller or the person called. People can tell when you are on a speaker phone because it is usually more difficult to hear and there is an echo. You may not want others to hear what you have to say. If you think you are on a speaker phone, ask the other person to pick up the phone. Say, "I'm having difficulty hearing you, Jack. Please pick up."

Being placed on a speaker phone also communicates a lack of interest in what you have to say when the other person is preoccupied with other tasks while speaking with you on a speaker phone.

Cellular telephones

Cellular telephone rings are disruptive in restaurants, meetings and other public places. Turn off and hide the cell phone out of view. It is inconsiderate to place a cell phone on the table. The message communicated is that you are more interested in waiting for someone to call than you are the dialogue you are having with your meal companion. Your companion will feel neglected and of low priority. Don't use a cell phone in the company of others unless the conversation pertains to them.

If you are expecting an urgent call, explain to your companion that you have your phone on vibrate and will accept only the urgent call. If it's necessary to make a call in front of someone, say, "I am here with so and so."

In a restaurant, meeting or theater, switch the cell phone to off and have your calls re-routed to your answering machine or service. If you are expecting a call, wear an apparatus that vibrates silently, excuse yourself, and take it privately. Another solution is to leave it switched on at the

reception desk of a restaurant—or, with the manager of
a theater, give your seat location. This means someone will
answer your call, come and
notify you, and you can take
the call in private. If you
have to make a call, excuse
yourself, go to where the cell
phone is being looked after,
and make your call there.

Beepers are worn by people
who must be accessible at all
times, such as doctors and
others who have critical emer-
gency situations. If it beeps in a public place, its owner must immediately turn it off and leave to take the call privately.

Whenever I receive a call from someone who is driving, I try to get off the
phone quickly. Pull off the road to use your cellular phone.

Facsimile

Facsimile messages should be kept as short as possible. Often, a "fax"
arriving at a central office location is read by others before your recipient
receives it. A facsimile is not recommended for anything personal or
potentially embarrassing. They are not suitable for invitations or thank
you letters.

Human felicity is produced not so much by great pieces of good fortune that seldom happen, as by little advantages that occur every day.

—Ben Franklin

Chapter 8

Effective Meetings

The best meetings are short and productive. Decide who needs to attend and notify them at least two to four weeks ahead. To save time, distribute the agenda in advance along with relevant material so that the participants will be prepared to give reports or bring information with them so that their thoughts and ideas can be heard.

Have a beginning and ending time—and stick to it. By always having a printed agenda, it will be easier to stick to the time schedule. When you prepare the agenda, gauge how much time to allow for each item. Keep a watch or clock on the table in front of you to help keep the meeting moving forward.

If an agenda item requires more time than you have allotted, appoint a sub-committee of two or three people to meet at another time. The sub-committee can discuss and investigate the issue and bring its findings to the next meeting.

The best time to schedule a meeting varies from one organization to another. Consider a sixty-minute, late-morning meeting—just before lunch or late afternoon, an hour before closing. That will help keep you to a time frame. Some organizations schedule meetings an hour before opening or at 5:00 p.m.

The meeting planner or chairperson should check the room in advance to see that it is clean, well lighted, and aired—with enough seating, water glasses, pads and pencils, and an agenda for each attendee.

With regard to a teleconference or a meeting conducted on a speaker phone, all participants should be introduced. A participant should speak only when addressed directly. (see Teleconferences Page 96).

Respond promptly to a meeting invitation. If you receive it via e-mail, check your calendar and send back a response immediately. Otherwise, you may forget to do so. When you have a contribution to make at a meeting, advise the chairperson in advance so that it can be included in the agenda.

Participants should arrive at meetings a few minutes early to prepare mentally and to review the agenda. Give yourself enough time to socialize and introduce yourself to newcomers.

If you are going to be unavoidably late to a meeting, call to advise the chairperson so that a decision can be made whether to go on without you. Advise the chairperson in advance if you have to leave early, so that your part of the agenda can be covered before you leave. Policy begins with the chairperson, who sets the example of being prompt. A "last minute person," rushing in at exactly the moment the meeting is to begin, is a late person. At the beginning of the meeting, the chairperson should make introductions of newcomers and others with their names, titles, responsibilities.

When you arrive, introduce yourself to other members and give your business card to the secretary. If you are a new member, wait to be assigned a seat. The chairs at either end of a conference table are for the two highest ranking members.

It's distracting to an audience and disrespectful to a speaker when people float in and out of meetings. If you know you can't stay for a meeting, stand in the back of the room for a few minutes. If you decide to sit down, stay for the entire meeting.

In a full-day program I presented for customer service representatives, the supervisor attended the meeting as a participant. She jumped up and left the meeting at least six times without a comment (she wasn't sick). The non-verbal message that the supervisor sent to her staff was that she didn't think the program had value. Contrast that with a supervisor from another organization who attended with representatives. She advised me before the program began that she had to leave the meeting at 11:45 a.m. to make a telephone call. When she returned, she came up to me on the lunch break and asked me to fill her in on what she had missed.

A latecomer should enter the meeting quietly, take a seat and listen. If refreshments have been served, the latecomer should wait until there is a break in the meeting to go to the buffet table.

When you want to air your views, keep your voice calm; let the other person finish talking before you speak. Avoid using the words *but* or *however* if you don't wish to be confrontational. Start your sentences with, "I see what you're saying, *and* I believe…" or, "That's an interesting idea, and it seems to me…." or, "Congratulations on a successful event, *and* I have some suggestions for next year."

Meeting Behavior

- Do take notes of the discussion. However, avoid doodling, which can be interpreted as not paying attention.

- Always ask permission before using a tape recorder.

- Don't interrupt anyone. If someone interrupts you, say, "Excuse me, I'm not finished."

- A side conversation while someone is speaking is rude.

- Ask for clarification for what you don't understand.

- Use collaborative language, say, "*We,*" not "*I.*"

- For example: "*We can send the order today*" or, "*Let's* see if we can find a solution to…"

- Be concise and stick to the subject.

- Don't distract from meetings by reading a newspaper or hammering away on a laptop.

- Delete slang speech habits from your conversation, such as "I'm like, ya know…" "Yeah," "Uh huh." Often, it's only by the sound of your voice that people know you. You don't want to sound immature or unprofessional.

If you are making a presentation, arrive up to an hour early. You'll have time to arrange and test equipment or visual aids, have printed material accessible, and give yourself time to go to the restroom. The extra time enables you to correct or compensate for glitches you may encounter such as a faulty electrical outlet or non-working microphone. You may have to rearrange chairs if you notice that you will be standing in front of a bank of windows that create a glare for the participants—in which case, they'll see only your outline, and squint during your presentation.

When you and a co-worker engage in a group meeting with a client, have your co-worker sit on the opposite side of the table if possible. You'll interact with other members of the group better. It will foster a more collaborative "we" feeling among all members. More information will also come to you through the body language of the members of the group if you and your co-worker sit in separate places. You and your partner will each be more observant of nods, subtle shifts in posture, and other signals that will give you information about your presentation.

At the end of a meeting, thank the chairperson and congratulate others who have made presentations.

Don't nibble while speaking. I have been at late afternoon meetings where bowls of snacks are on the table. At one meeting, it was difficult to take a highly paid consultant's words seriously. He slouched in his chair, and he spoke in a nonchalant manner while nibbling on snacks. As it turned out, his advice matched his manners. It was bad, and following it was a colossal error.

Robert's Rules of Order is the bible for meeting protocol. To give you added confidence as a chairperson, meeting planner, or participant, you will find organizations such as Toastmasters are invaluable. Also inquire whether your organization, local college, or chamber of commerce offers programs in leadership and public speaking. The National Association of

Parliamentarians, a non-profit organization, has chapters throughout the U.S. and in other countries. It provides services to the business community by offering educational seminars, reference material and professional assistance.

National Association of Parliamentarians
213 South Main Street
Independence, MO 64050-3850
(816) 833-3892
(888) NAP-2929
E-mail: hq@nap2.org
Web site: www.parliamentarians.org/parlipro.htm

Toastmasters International
Web site: www.toastmasters.org

Make a positive impression at your company's off-site meeting. Remember this is still business. Your demeanor is just as important at an off-site meeting as it is at home quarters. Dress appropriately for all events. Even though the attire may be casual, it should be smart casual. Ask the meeting planner if you'll need a jacket and dress shoes for the dining room, and whether ties or sweaters are appropriate for meetings.

Mingle, not just with co-workers, but others who are in attendance. Make it a point, at meetings and during meals, to sit next to people you don't know well. Attend and participate in all sessions. Don't skip out thinking you won't be missed. Focus on the event and socialize with attendees. Keep cell phone usage to a minimum.

Teleconferences (Audioconferences)

The social courtesies of a public meeting are applied to teleconference calls. Participants should be notified at least a few days before the call, agendas sent with a participant list; with call start and end times specified. Designate someone to take and distribute notes of the conference call.

Participants should schedule uninterrupted time in a quiet location, review the agenda, and be on time for the call. If it's necessary to use a cell phone, find a fixed spot and ensure a strong signal. Introduce yourself each time you speak ("This is Taylor…").

Avoid side conversations. Everyone should give the moderator full attention while the moderator guides the call through the agenda.

The moderator introduces each participant at the beginning of the call. Let callers know when questions and comments may be offered (at any time during the call or at a specified time). Make sure everyone has a chance to speak. When presenting information, give others regular opportunities to ask questions or make clarifications. Before ending the call, review who is assigned to which tasks along with deadlines as needed. Send out notes from the call to all participants. Include the date and time of the next scheduled call if known.

As we advance in the use of technology, videoconferences, where participants hear and see those in other sites, will be more commonplace. The visual advantage will make us even more aware of professional presence, body language, facial expressions, gestures, and mannerisms.

> *Gratitude is a spiritual state, an acknowledgement of our own unimportance and dependence on others.*
> —Connie Leas, The Art of Thank You

Chapter 9

Letter Writing to Thank, Acknowledge and Build Rapport

Your career can reap dividends from a timely letter or note. Conversely, an omission of an expected letter or acknowledgment can negate a budding relationship, and you may never know why.

A handwritten personal note is tangible. You can hold it, re-read it and save it. People rarely save e-mail or faxed thank-you notes. I was recently a guest speaker at a meeting of the Human Resource Association. During lunch, several of us were discussing the value of a thank-you note or letter, written or typed, on a correspondence card versus an e-mail thank-you. A human resource manager for an accounting firm said he is impressed when a job applicant takes the time to send a thank-you note. Then he added, "After sending a thank-you note through the postal service, an applicant can follow-up in a few days with an e-mail message. That way, I can respond quickly about the status of the application."

Writing notes and letters is a way to connect you with customers, clients and friends. Employees can be motivated by letters of appreciation and recognition of their efforts.

You might wonder whether writing a letter or note is necessary since we have e-mail and facsimile. After all, technology has made communication so much faster. Yet, people with whom I speak are impressed when they receive a personal note.

I was told that the following thank you letter written to the Cincinnati Opera Association was greatly appreciated.

Dear Christopher Milligan,

Thank you for reviewing for the Town Club members the exciting upcoming Cincinnati opera season. Since it was our last meeting before the move to the Bankers Club, I was apprehensive about how it was all going to work. I needn't have had any fear. You presented an interesting, enlightening program in the midst of all the chaos.

I received many comments from our members about how much they enjoyed the program and talented performances of Jeffrey and Tina and their accompanist, Carol. Please convey our thanks to them.

You have many admirers and supporters who are members of the Town Club. You added to that number today.

Sincerely,
Marja Barrett

Why did it make a favorable impression? Here are some of the reasons:

- **It was timely, sent immediately after the program.**
- **It thanked the performers for a fine presentation.**
- **It was personalized and included the names of the performers.**
- **It was complimentary in acknowledging the challenges they had to overcome.**
- **It gave assurance that their efforts would be rewarded.**

Personal notes add a human touch in a world of global competition and technology. A personal note stands out from the daily deluge of electronic messages and computerized form letters. Many people tell me that the first letters that they open are the ones that are hand addressed. It's a way of saying, "You are important."

Personal notes and letters keep your connections to friends and business associates alive. A thank-you note after an interview, whether or not you get the order, is sure to impress. A thank-you note written to a customer can encourage repeat orders. Connect with people you meet at business meetings by sending warm notes that say, "I enjoyed meeting you at…" A timely note can lead to additional business or referrals. Send notes to friends and relations who have been supportive.

Write notes on letterhead or handwrite them on correspondence cards when someone gives you a gift. A note is welcome after a dinner or cocktail party. Written responses are appropriate for written invitations. Send a note anytime someone goes out of the way to help you. Send a congratulatory note when a friend or colleague is promoted or receives recognition for outstanding contributions to the community.

A recipient will tell others. A note of appreciation to a CEO praising a staff member who went the extra mile for me during a difficult period of my life was read at a weekly staff meeting. It takes a little more time, thought and caring to compose a letter of appreciation, and that's exactly why it's valued.

Send a pre-printed card when a business associate marries as well as for celebrations such as the birth of a child or a Bar Mitzvah or Bat Mitzvah. Always add a personal note to pre-printed cards and sign them. I'll never forget the disappointment of a friend who received a birthday card from his regional manager who had not personally signed the card. My friend interpreted the card as an empty gesture.

A condolence note should be handwritten. Send a note if you were a friend or associate of either the deceased or survivor. We all want our loved ones to be remembered in a loving manner. Include a personal remembrance about the deceased in your note.

When you meet new business associates, send notes saying how nice it was to meet them. Send a congratulatory note or card to a retiree. If someone has lost a job, send a note and extend an invitation to meet for lunch and offer encouragement.

In recognizing kindness and other people's achievements, you are truly the one who will reap benefits because you will experience the joy of gratitude in your own heart.

How to write it

Make a draft of what you want to say in your letter. Use scratch paper to compose your thoughts and write conversationally. Imagine you are speaking to the person to whom you are writing. Keep it brief. Don't use jargon or complicated language. Read it aloud, and check the grammar and spelling. Have someone proof read your letter and double check spelling, including the name.

Write your letter neatly on good-quality paper stock with a letterhead. Your letter should be free of correction marks and crossed-out words.

Begin your letter with a salutation: *Dear Mr. Rowland* or *Dear Ms. Goshen*—unless you are on a first-name basis. If you are not sure whether you are writing to a man or woman, use the full name, such as, *Dear Dorsey Jones*. In more formal business letters, avoid stereotypical language such as Dear Sir, which excludes women. *To whom it may concern* is too impersonal. Your letter will receive more attention if you address it to a person. Endeavor to get a name by making a telephone call or check out the company's web site. If you can't find a person to whom you can send your letter, address it to the department, for example, *To Customer Service*.

Your complimentary close will depend upon your relationship with the recipient. More formal closings are *Sincerely, Sincerely yours, Cordially* or *Yours truly*. The closing for a friend is less formal: *Best wishes, Best regards, Regards, Warm regards*. Avoid using *Affectionately* and *Fondly* in your business correspondence. *Respectfully* or *Most respectfully* is very formal and used when writing to the president of the United States and religious officials such as an archbishop or bishop.

Notes may be handwritten on correspondence cards or fold-over note cards with your company name or logo. Cards with your own name may be handwritten for personal notes.

- **Write the date correctly: December 12, 2008.   Except for postcards, don't write 12/12/08 or 12.12.08.**
- **The inside address includes titles that are spelled out, that is,**
  Debbie Simpson, President (not Pres.)
  Jan Givens, Manager (not Mgr.)
- **M.D., R.N., Ph.D. are abbreviated.**
- **Follow guidelines of the U.S. Post Office in addressing envelopes. Use numerals for numbered streets; i.e., 10th Street or 1st Street.**
- **Traditional formal correspondence does not use abbreviations for "Street," "Avenue," "Parkway," "Road," or state names.**
- **Write out city names.**
- **Include 9 numerals ZIP.**

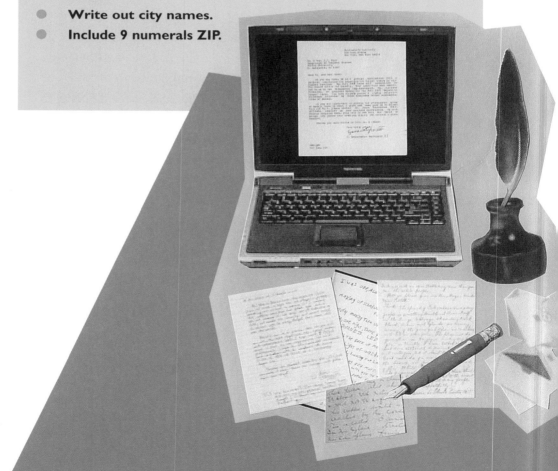

Sample letters you can use as models.

Thank you note after having dinner in someone's home:

Dear Maxine,

Thank you for an elegant evening. Chris and I were so happy to be included in the inauguration of your beautiful newly decorated dining room.

The meal was magnificent. Ralph's pesto appetizer was delicious. The Mediterranean vegetable salad was a wonderful complement to the lamb. And the chocolate brownies and lemon bars were a perfect ending.

You have an interesting and diverse group of friends. We all were having such a good time that no one wanted the evening to end.

Chris and I look forward to seeing you and Ralph soon.

Affectionately,
Shelly

Thank you for a gift:

Dear Vernon,

Thank you for the elegant crystal paperweight. It looks splendid on my desk. Each time I look at it, I'm reminded of you and our long-time friendship.

I'm so glad you had time to visit us when you were in Little Rock. Hopefully, we'll be able to see you again in August when we are in Boston for the Rotary Conference.

Best wishes to you and Betty,
Louis

Dear Allison,

Thank you for the delicious gift box of pears. How did you know that pears are my favorite fruit? The gift box also included a booklet of pear recipes. Last evening, our family enjoyed jewel pear salad. It was the best part of our meal. Your gift of "health" is greatly appreciated by all of us.

Best holiday wishes to you and
your family,
Tracy

Thank you for a referral

Dear Dan,

Thank you for referring me to Ned Hertzenberg at the Cincinnati Scholarship Foundation. We met this morning, and the prospects of being hired look good. Another interview is scheduled for next Wednesday. I'll keep you posted.

You're a great friend.
Warm regards,
Katie Sanderson

Congratulations

Dear Edwin,

Congratulations on receiving the Distinguished Leadership Award. Your leadership and contributions have made a big difference in our community. I think about how you spearheaded the campaign to have the National Underground Railroad Freedom Center built in Cincinnati eleven years ago, and now that vision is a reality.

The Freedom Center will have an impact locally and nationally. The honor is so well deserved. We all applaud your accomplishments.

Sincerely,
Marja Barrett

Letter of Apology

A sincere letter of apology or verbal apology is an opportunity to create good will and keep your friend, client or customer. Write it immediately to soften hurt feelings.

Apologies are made to clients or customers who are dissatisfied with a product or service. Other occasions to apologize are when you forgot an appointment, or you forgot to RSVP to a personal invitation or forgot to attend an event, or have had too much to drink at a gathering.

Dear Mrs. White:

Thank you for writing us about the incident in our store. We regret that you were inconvenienced. Please accept our apology.

We appreciate your writing to us so that we may correct this situation. We shall endeavor to provide the service that you expect.

Sincerely,
Scott Ward, Manager

Dear Jack,

Please accept my apology for not notifying you of the postponement of this morning's meeting. The meeting will be held on October 5 at 9:00 a.m.

I'm sorry my oversight caused you inconvenience and hope you will accept my apology.

Sincerely,
Grace Rush

Letters of Condolence

Letters of condolence may be penned on plain white note paper. Including a fond remembrance of the deceased is comforting to the bereaved. If you send a pre-printed card, add a short personal note such as "Our thoughts and prayers are with you and your family."

Dear Tom,

Ron and I were deeply saddened to hear about Carolyn's death. We will greatly miss her friendship and loving generous heart.

Please call us if there is anything we can do. Ron and I are always available.

Love,
Lisa

Letter to acknowledge sympathy

When someone sends flowers or a letter of condolence, it is appropriate to send a personal penned note of thank you. The note can be brief, such as, "Thank you for the beautiful flowers" or "Thank you for your kindness." When pre-printed notes are used, add a penned note for personal acquaintances. Write personal notes to family members and friends who have written letters or sent flowers.

When you sign a letter or note as a couple, the name of the person who writes the note is last.

Handwritten versus typed notes depend on penmanship. If your handwriting is illegible, a typed note is acceptable. However, make the attempt to handwrite short notes.

Chapter 10

The Art of Gift Giving

The art of gift giving has been around for a long time. The late professional wrestler "Flyin' Brian" Pillman and I were guests on a local cable television show. Brian was making an appearance to warn teenagers about the dangers of drugs, and I was invited to give tips on business etiquette. The host interviewed both of us immediately after a short video clip featuring Brian winning a wrestling match. The host turned to me and said, "Marja, do you have any etiquette tips for Brian?" Of course, we all began to laugh. Whew! I thought. What am I supposed to say to Brian? There I sat next to this beautiful man with long blonde curls and muscles coming out of his jacket and I was speechless. My initial response was not to be critical of him because he was so physically strong, and so our discussion led to how to pay deference.

It was to the strong man that our primitive ancestors first paid deference. Gifts were given to the strongest and most powerful person of the tribe, who could protect the community. People would pay deference by bringing gifts to assure their safety from enemies and ferocious animals. He was their hero. Deference was also paid to elders—because they were the wise sages and vessels who contained the stories of the tribe and passed them from one generation to another.

Today, we give gifts for a variety of reasons. It's an excellent way to make a personal connection or cement a relationship with a customer or client. Gift giving keeps a business relationship alive.

In addition to giving gifts to build and maintain personal and business relationships, we give gifts to promote products or services, to show appreciation, to express an apology, to encourage, to congratulate or to celebrate. A gift may be given to a new client at the signing of a contract. If someone goes out of the way to help you, consider giving a gift in appreciation.

Selecting an appropriate gift requires knowledge and sensitivity. Before sending a gift, inquire if the recipient company has guidelines or any restrictions about gift giving. Some companies prohibit employees from accepting any gifts. Others limit value to twenty-five dollars. Contact the personnel department to request guidelines or ask your client directly.

It is not appropriate to give an expensive gift to someone with whom you are negotiating a business deal, as it could be interpreted as a bribe for their business. Giving cash to a client can also have bribery overtones. A gift that is too expensive could alienate a client. And avoid gifts to business associates that can be taken the wrong way. Never give lingerie to the opposite sex or a gift that will embarrass the recipient. A gift with religious connotations can also offend. Give liquor only if you know the recipient will appreciate it.

A gift does not have to be expensive to make a favorable impression on a client. Gifts should reflect your business and be in good taste. Giving a gift to a client should not be seen as an advertising tactic with your logo prominently displayed. Forego logos on gifts unless they are small and subtle. The gift should be something that reminds the recipient of your company each time it is used.

When selecting a gift, think about your client's specific interests and preferences such as type of music, sports, or hobbies. Acceptable gifts can be office related, such as paperweights, calendars, bookends, pens, plants, food baskets, gift certificates, magazine subscriptions and books. A box of wrapped chocolates or cookies can be used in the office or taken home. A flower bouquet or beautiful plant is appropriate when you wish to thank, congratulate, or mark a milestone such as your customer's grand opening or an anniversary celebration.

Select top-quality, non-denominational holiday cards that reflect the spirit of the season with a general message such as Season's Greetings, Greetings of Peace, Happy Holidays or Happy New Year. Avoid Santa images and religious cards unless you know the recipient's religious affiliation. Client relationships are strengthened when you and your staff add your personal signatures to cards. A greeting card with only the company name printed on it is too impersonal. Electronic greeting cards are not appropriate for business use. To communicate warmth, handwrite names and addresses and use holiday postage stamps, not a meter stamp.

Gift giving can be expensive. How much you spend is based on the number of customers and clients. To keep it affordable, send gifts to the best customers and send cards personally signed to the rest. Always choose quality gifts, even with a small budget. Consider giving a small, elegant twenty-five dollar gift that will be well received instead of a lavish gift.

Sending a birthday card to a client, secretary or assistant may make a bigger impression than a gift. Remembering spouses and children show that you care about the person. A good friend gives the gift of time to customers she knows well. She offers to take their children to dinner, a movie, and a drive to see the holiday lights.

If a gift is returned to the giver, it should be done within twenty-four hours with a note of thanks for the gesture and an explanation stating that the company has certain guidelines for accepting gifts.

If you're looking for a quantity of gifts, place your order six to eight weeks in advance as many companies need a lead time to process large orders.

Keep a file of hobbies and interests of clients, employees and friends that you wish to acknowledge with personal gifts. Generally, when giving gifts to your office employees, it's best to give everyone the same gifts so that there are no comparisons or hurt feelings. If you wish to reward an employee with a more expensive gift for extraordinary service, do so privately.

A well-meaning supervisor invited ten of his staff members to dinner at a local restaurant during the holidays. He was disappointed that no one mentioned it the next day, not even a verbal thank-you. What happened? The supervisor's intentions were good. He wanted to show his appreciation. However, he did not take into account their preferences during the busy holiday season. Chances are that the employees felt that the dinner extended their work day and took them away from their families (spouses were not included). A catered lunch, restaurant gift certificates or gift baskets would have been better received.

Consider a donation in the client's name to his favorite charity. An acknowledgement can be sent stating that a donation was made in his name. However, don't specify the amount. Most charities will send a nice note for you.

You can buy gifts and, without spending any more money than the cost of the gifts, donate to charities at the same time. GreaterGood.com, which is owned by the Hunger Site Network, represents over one hundred leading merchants that will donate up to fifteen percent of gift costs to charities of your choice. GreaterGood.com represents bookstores, clothing stores, food companies, sporting goods stores and many others.

Consider a gift of a tree planted in the recipient's name. I recently honored a friend who left our city by donating a Freedom Tree in his name to a local park. A portion of the cost of the tree was donated to the National Underground Railroad Freedom Center in Cincinnati. He received a certificate, and I included a note of best wishes and added: "You have roots here." The web site for Freedom Trees is www.freedomtrees.com

Keep your eyes open throughout the year for business and personal gift ideas. I enjoy picking up unusual and interesting gifts for family, friends and business associates while traveling. When you see something that you know a person on your gift list will like, buy it and present it at the appropriate time.

Keep on hand a selection of pre-wrapped items for those who have hosted you in their homes and for birthday and thank-you gifts. It will save you from rushing around at the last minute. Hand-made gifts and home-made edibles are especially appreciated.

Unique wrapping can make even a small present stand out. Include a hand-written note and, if possible, deliver your gifts in person.

Accolades go to companies who encourage and support their employees giving back to the community through their donation of time and talents, whether serving on committees and boards in the community or encouraging special projects. It's a chance for employees to give back. At Pomeroy IT Solutions, Inc., volunteerism and giving back to the community is fostered among all employees. Its main charity is the Boomer Esiason Foundation for Cystic Fibrosis. The employees also built and sponsored a home with Habitat for Humanity.

Chapter 11

Business Entertaining

When it is advantageous to get to know your customers and clients on a deeper level, entertaining them is the best way to do this. Of course, you can give them tickets to a ballgame or a symphony. However, it is not the same as inviting them to join you for a ballgame, symphony or lunch. When people are relaxed and enjoying themselves, they open up. You learn more about one another and build stronger bonds. It's a time to listen for cues that will help you provide better service to your clients. For example, business entertaining frequently takes on a more social nature and very little or no business is discussed. Instead, discussion centers on mutual interests of family, travel, sports or hobbies.

If you are uncomfortable in social settings, you will be petrified at the thought of entertaining or accepting invitations. The greatest rewards come from going beyond your comfort zone. My first client, an exceptionally gifted businesswoman, felt as if she dropped the ball when she refused a significant business lunch invitation from the president of her

company. She did not tell the president that she declined the invitation because she was concerned that she did not know which utensils to use in a formal setting of an upscale dining establishment. After several business etiquette and protocol sessions, she had confidence to coordinate special events for her company on a local and national level. The last time I spoke with her, she was involved in politics and anticipated attending banquets in Washington, D.C., and had started her own video production company.

Polished social skills will help you to successfully navigate your way through business and social situations. It's all about forgetting yourself and making your guest feel comfortable whether you are in a white table-cloth restaurant or a mom and pop establishment. It is not showing off or acting superior to others. The person with gracious social skills is pleasant to be around because she is at ease and puts others at ease.

Take the mystery out of business entertaining so that you can have more enjoyment with clients, co-workers, family and friends. Look at it as a journey because you will continue to learn after you have finished these chapters, and your life will be enriched.

When you are the Host

Extending Invitations

Business is accomplished over lunch as well as venues such as the golf course. An invitation to lunch may be made by telephone. You should place the call yourself and not ask your secretary to extend the invitation. Make it clear to your client that you are hosting by saying something like, "I'd like you to be my guest at lunch to discuss some ideas about the project."

Where does your client like to eat? Contact someone such as the secretary to find out. Otherwise, offer a choice of two restaurants in convenient locations to both of you. It helps if you are familiar with the menus and you know your client's food preferences. Does your client enjoy seafood? If a client is vegetarian, go to a restaurant that offers a versatile menu. Verify the time and exact location of the restaurant with your guest, as well as the name under which you make the reservation.

Making Reservations

Call the restaurant for availability before you invite your guest. After you invite your guest, call the restaurant back to confirm your reservation. It's important to have reservations even if it's a spur-of-the-moment luncheon invitation. By doing so, you will receive better service and recognition. You won't be kept waiting or be turned away because a private party has taken over the whole facility. It's also disruptive to a busy and smooth running establishment to hastily set up a suitable table because you didn't make a reservation.

Specify the number of people and give other information that will help the restaurant staff give you excellent service such as inquiring about vegetarian meals.   Before you hang up, ask for the name of the person who takes your reservation. If there is a question about your reservation when you arrive, you have the name of the person with whom you spoke. Remember to call the restaurant if you need to change the time or cancel your reservation. Also call in advance if the number of attendees increases or decreases so that the appropriate table will be reserved. This is also the time to advise if space for a wheelchair is needed.

Your table location in a restaurant is important. Keep in mind the purpose of your meeting is to discuss business, to speak and hear one another easily. If you are familiar with the restaurant, you can specify the area in which you wish to sit. You don't want to sit next to the kitchen, busy aisle, noise or loud music. You'll not be able to converse at all if you are placed next to a group of twenty birthday party revelers.

Be polite and practice humility when making requests. Say, "If at all possible, may I request a table on the window?" Respect the restaurant business. Don't tell people what you want or make commands. Make requests courteously. Respect for others goes a long way.

Jacqueline Kennedy was known for her gracious manner when making requests. She would use phrases such as "May I have...?" and "Could you please help me...?" People enjoyed serving her.

Make a connection. If you are having an important meeting and the restaurant is unfamiliar, visit it a day ahead and introduce yourself and tell who is going to be there. If you think it will take a gratuity, by all means, give one. At this initial visit, you can make special arrangements for the payment of the bill.

Luncheon at your office

A luncheon at your office can be special, quiet and private. If you bring food in, remove it from take-out cartons and serve it on attractive china, serve beverages in goblets, use attractive cups and saucers, cloth or quality paper napkins, stainless steel or silver-plate utensils. Place the plates of food and sandwiches nearest your guests. Serve your guests first. The home team should not reach across people for food.

Pause, relax and enjoy your food and chit-chat for a few minutes before you discuss business. Inform your staff not to disturb you with telephone calls. It is rude to interrupt your meeting by taking a call unless it concerns everyone in the meeting or it is an emergency.

If your organization has an attractive private employee dining room, invite your client to join you for lunch. It will be a special treat for your guest and an opportunity for you to introduce your company's VIPs.

Private Club

A private club is preferred by many because checks can be signed discreetly and gratuities are automatically added to the bill. You are known by the staff and addressed by your name in a respectful manner.

Assure Success

As the host, you set the tone of your luncheon. You want to assure your guest's comfort. The morning of your luncheon, call your client and say that you are looking forward to the lunch engagement. Confirm the time and place to avoid a misunderstanding. It's also a good idea to confirm your restaurant reservation.

In addition, how much time are you allowing for lunch? Does your client have to be back in the office within an hour or is this going to be a more leisurely lunch? If your client needs to be back in the office at 1:15 p.m. for a meeting, then you'll have to keep things moving. When there are time constraints, say to the server before the specials are mentioned, "We need to make our selection quickly because we have a lot to discuss." Hopefully, this will also cut down on unnecessary interruptions. These are points to address so that you accomplish what you want in the allotted time.

Be early to greet your client at the restaurant. It is rude to keep your guest waiting. If you have never met, suggest a specific place to meet, such as, next to the statue. Alternatively, you may be seated and ask that your guest be brought to your table. Give the maitre d' your guest's name. Rise from the table to greet your guest.

By arriving fifteen minutes early you can check on your table location and give the maitre d' last minute instructions. This is a good time to arrange for payment. If you use a credit card, give it to the cashier so that you don't have to scramble for it later. It's a good idea to carry two cards in case one is not accepted or has expired. If you are near your limit, call and check with the credit card company.

You may order a beverage while you are waiting for your client. If you've waited twenty minutes, place a call to your client's office just in case something has happened. If your guest does not come, you may leave or remain and have lunch. If you choose to leave, tip the server because you have occupied a table, thus preventing another person from being served.

Seating

You can put your guest at ease by taking the lead. Offer your guest the preferred seat with room or window view. However, the host should sit where he can easily summon the server. In the business world, it does not automatically mean that the woman or first person at the table sits in the chair that the maitre d' offers. We defer to the higher ranking person, our clients and to other guests. Your client will feel comfortable if you say, "Why don't you sit here so you have the river view." You can also give your client a choice of seats. Some people are light sensitive and may prefer sitting with their back to the window. (See Social Courtesies Chapter 2).

Be observant of anything that will distract from your conversation such as a palm tree too close to the chair of your guest, a centerpiece obstructing your view of each other (remove it or place it to the side), a wobbly table, a cold draft or audio system above your table (request another table).

Ordering Food and Beverage

Once you are seated, beverage orders are taken and the napkin is removed from the table and placed in the lap. Offer your guests a choice of beverages. If one chooses not to drink an alcoholic beverage, simply order juice, bottled water or iced tea. Coffee is usually not ordered until the end of the meal unless it is a frosty day.

In a formal restaurant, your guest is given a menu first. If this doesn't happen, you can pass your menu to your guest. You can give additional cues to the wait staff that you are the host by saying, "My guest will order first."

Quickly look over the menu and make your choice. It's helpful to the guest if the host makes one or two recommendations from the menu. After the recommendations, invite your guest to order. The host orders last. Closing the menu and placing it on the table is a signal for the server to take your orders.

Kind of food to order at a business lunch

It's difficult to have a conversation with someone who is constantly looking down at their food. In order to make eye-contact while you converse, select food that is simple to eat and doesn't require concentration. At formal meals, avoid ordering messy foods, difficult-to-eat foods like hamburgers, corn on the cob and tacos. Save the ribs and pasta for those times you are with your friends and family. Lighter food is appropriate for lunch and that includes main course salads.

When you are dining with others, try to order similar food. If you are the only one to order a first course such as soup, the other guests may not be served until you finish your soup. Your companions will watch you eat your soup and think "If Darryl hadn't ordered soup, we'd have our sandwiches by now." You can easily adjust your order by saying, "Please bring my soup at the same time that everyone is served their food," or you can cancel it. Incidentally, soup is a good luncheon choice, providing you eat it properly, because there's less fuss and no cutting.

If there are eight or more diners, consider a set menu so that the meals will all be served at the same time. Entertaining with a set menu can also save you money. Do take into consideration any dietary requirements of your guests.

Conversation

It's the host's responsibility to take charge of conversation to make guests feel at ease. Business is usually not discussed until after orders are placed or entrees are finished. It's up to the host to bring up the topic of business. However, it's appropriate to oblige a customer who brings up the topic of business sooner than you expected. The first ten minutes or so is usually light conversation.   Be prepared with two or three topics or ideas that you can add to the conversation. Spending a few minutes in preparation for your meeting will pay dividends. Focus on your companion and the discussion. Don't look around to see who's coming into the restaurant. (How to converse, and appropriate and inappropriate topics of conversation are covered in Chapter 4).

The Host leads

The guest seated to the right of the host is served first, the host is served last.   Usually everyone is served before the host gives the cue to begin eating. However, if there are many people seated at the table, the host may say, "Please, begin eating while your food is hot."

As the host, serve food and pass rolls to guests before helping yourself. Do ask your guest questions about the food like, "How is your salmon?" If you notice that a guest's quiche is burnt on the bottom, signal your server and invite your guest to order something else. It is, however, important to keep your focus on your meeting. If you have been served your filet mignon medium instead of rare, it is less distracting to your meeting if you don't send it back.

Always, always treat servers respectfully. It is disturbing to guests when the host berates a server. If there is something amiss, quietly signal your server and have it corrected. If it is a serious matter, excuse yourself from the table and see a manager. You can also send a letter to the manager expressing your dissatisfaction.

Paying the bill

When the meal is over, the host places the napkin on the table and requests the check. The payment of your meal should be done quietly and inconspicuously. Think about the guest in your home where there are no monetary transactions and how that feels to you and your guest. You want to approximate that as closely as possible when you entertain in restaurants.

You can simulate this atmosphere by refraining from taking out your bill-fold in front of guests at the table. It detracts from the ambiance of the occasion and makes guests feel uneasy when the host refers to the check and figures out the gratuity in their presence. This is not the place to scrutinize the bill. Do a quick tip calculation—20 percent is easiest (.20 x total before tax).

If you are entertaining a group in a public restaurant, you can request that the check not be brought to the table. During dessert, excuse yourself as though going to the washroom, pay the cashier, include the gratuity if it has not already been added, and return to your table to continue your conversation. This is especially helpful if you have a client who is uncomfortable with your paying the check.

If the check is brought to the table or inadvertently given to your guest, pick it up immediately, otherwise, your guest will not hear another word of your conversation. Instead, he will be thinking about whether to pick up the check or offer to pay half. If your guest grabs the check, extend your hand and politely say, "Art, this is my treat." If he persists say, "You can treat next time." This is more challenging to accomplish if the client is an older man being treated by a woman, especially if the client is affluent or a macho type.

When you are the Guest

A guest demonstrates graciousness by being prompt, prepared and dressed appropriately for the meeting. You'll feel refreshed and composed by arriving a few minutes early to use the washroom. If you are joining a group, first greet your host and then the other guests. Your host may wish to assign seats, so pause a moment at the table rather than sit down immediately.

If you are unexpectedly delayed, call the restaurant and have a message delivered to your host. When you arrive, join your group at whatever course is being served, even if it's just coffee, so that you do not delay the meeting.

If the host makes recommendations from the menu, it is a compliment to order a recommended dish. When the server takes the order, you may ask how a dish is prepared. However, don't ask to sample food before you order.

You'll feel empowered if you spend a few minutes to prepare for your luncheon. Know the purpose of the meeting and what is expected of you and who else is invited. Take along two or three ideas to add to the conversation.

It's inappropriate for a guest to ask to bring an uninvited person to a luncheon as it could disrupt the business nature of the conversation.

The morning I confirmed a luncheon appointment with a business associate, she asked if she could bring a longtime friend who was in town for the day. I agreed. However, we did not accomplish the business of which I had hoped in this scenario. It's best if the host reschedules the appointment by saying, "Let's have lunch another day. I'm sure you and your friend will have a lot of catching-up to do." And your business associate will be most grateful.

Habits

I think it's important to be aware of habits that detract from one's professionalism at the table. It's seldom noticed if one picks up the wrong fork. However, it is noticeable to slouch in the chair, reach across the table for the salt instead of saying, "Please pass the salt and pepper." Don't speak boisterously, monopolize the conversation, or make noise with utensils, while drinking beverages or eating soup. It's not about food—it's a meeting!

Thanking your Host

At the end of the meal, thank your host. However, do not say, "Thanks for the meal." Thank your host for the main purpose of the event, that is, an enjoyable time, the opportunity to meet the new dean of the law school, marketing director, or the opportunity to brainstorm on a topic. You can be complimentary about the food by saying something like, "The food was delicious."

It's easier to write a thank-you note to your host as soon as you return to your office while the conversation is fresh in your mind. (See Letter Writing, Chapter 9).

Dutch-treat

When you invite someone to go to lunch or other entertainment, the usual assumption is that whoever invites, pays. But, there are times when you may wish to have an outing with friends. It should be made very clear when you extend the invitation that you'll all go Dutch.

If you are invited to lunch and are uncomfortable with the other person paying the tab, you can say to your companion at the restaurant, "Let's request separate checks."

If a group shares the check, it's best to divide it evenly rather than try to figure out what each person ordered. If you order the most expensive dish or beverages, offer to pay the extra cost so that the bill is not excessive for your companions. It is considerate to order meals of similar cost.

Dutch-treat shock: A co-worker invited two other couples to join him and his wife for a weekend at their vacation home on a lake. All happily accepted and had a wonderful time until the end of the weekend when the host gave each couple a bill for two hundred dollars, their share of the weekend expenses. That was the first they knew that they would pay for anything. The co-workers probably would have been happy to share in the costs if the host had made that clear when he invited them. The co-workers could also have asked if they could contribute when they accepted the invitation.

Wine Etiquette

Ordering wine need not be intimidating. It is better to ask for a recommendation from a knowledgeable person or staff member than to show your lack of knowledge of wine by choosing inappropriately. You needn't order the most expensive wine on the list. The wine steward will give several choices in different price ranges. Indicate your preference. If one of your guests is a wine connoisseur, you might invite her to choose the wine. If you are serving a set menu, you can also select the wine prior to the dinner. Champagne goes with everything and makes an occasion special.

Pairing red wine with red meats and white wines with fish and fowl does not apply as it did years ago. The wine should complement the food. Lighter wines are served with lighter foods whether they are red or white. More complex wines are served with richer dishes.

When the wine steward presents the bottle to the host, the label is checked to verify that it was the wine ordered. After the cork is removed, it is placed in front of the host. It is not necessary to smell the cork. It is presented so that you may check to ensure the wine did not come into contact with air, which could spoil it. If a wine stain runs from one end of the cork to the other, chances are it is spoiled. The wine steward will pour a taste for the host, who then nods his head in approval. Guests are served first with the host being served last. Refuse a bottle of wine only if you are absolutely sure it is spoiled.

As a guest, never help yourself to wine unless invited to do so. It is inappropriate to order a cocktail if the host has offered guests a special wine. If you do not wish to drink alcohol, quietly say, "No thank-you." A thoughtful host will also offer a non-alcoholic beverage.

Toasts

Toasts are drunk and speeches are usually given after dessert is served at formal luncheons, dinners and banquets, and occasionally before dinner.

Toasts are made with wine or any beverage you have in front of you. If you don't drink alcohol, you may just lift the glass to your lips. Or if your glasses are removed, the gesture is pantomimed by lifting your hand as though holding a glass. After the host proposes the first toast, other guests may do so.

The host of a dinner stands and offers the first toast. Other guests do not stand unless the person being toasted is revered.

The best toasts are brief, said in one or two sentences or not longer than one or two minutes. A toast should come from the heart. Toasts can be gracious, humorous, sentimental, nostalgic, but not smutty or offensive in any way. Avoid politics, religion and humor that will embarrass the person being toasted. Address your remarks about the person being toasted to everyone. After your remarks, look at the person being toasted and nod your head before sipping.

If you are the one being toasted, do not lift your glass to toast yourself. After you are toasted, immediately stand and thank the hosts and guests and toast them in return. At a banquet, there is usually a master of ceremonies who proposes the toasts; otherwise they are proposed by the company president. If you are a dinner guest where toasts have not been proposed, but you would like to propose one to thank the host, you must ask the host's permission.

A momentary lapse in good taste can backfire. A prospective member was denied membership in a prestigious country club. A member was offended by a toast he had proposed at a function. When I heard this story, I was shocked. I knew him and thought that any organization would have been lucky to have him as a member. In this case, he made a negative first impression by giving a toast not deemed proper by one decision maker.

Final interviews for positions often include a meal. You will feel more comfortable by practicing and being aware of how to be a gracious host and gracious guest.

The Gracious Host

Provides a comfortable setting

Extends invitation

Selects restaurant

Arrives early to greet guests

Confirms reservations at
restaurant

Assigns seats

Visits or calls restaurant in
advance to select table, give
special instructions

Has impeccable table manners

Makes introductions

Is complimentary

Recommends house specialties

Is aware of guest's dietary
restrictions

Initiates conversation

Proposes toast

Invites guest to order first

Serves guest first

Gives cues when meal begins and
ends

Pays bill, gratuity, cloak room

The Gracious Guest

Responds promptly and
enthusiastically to invitation

Doesn't cancel except for emergency

Is prompt for the occasion

Knows purpose of event

Waits to be assigned a seat

Doesn't bring uninvited guest

Dresses appropriately

Has impeccable table manners

Orders food that is simple to eat

Is complimentary

Takes cue from host when ordering

Doesn't over-indulge (food or drink)

Participates in conversation

Doesn't complain

Greets guest of honor and hosts
before helping oneself to food

Doesn't overload plate

Doesn't groom oneself at table

Thanks host before leaving and sends
a thank-you note

Eat, Drink and Be Mannerly

Formal and informal meals involve multiple courses. The first course is usually an appetizer such as seafood cocktail or soup. This course may be followed by the salad and entrée. Sorbet, a fruit ice to cleanse the palate, is served between courses in small chilled glasses. Dessert and coffee follow the entrée after dishes are removed.

A formal place setting consists of a service plate or charger, napkin, stemware, utensils, and often a bread and butter plate. At formal dinners, there are not more than three forks and three knives and a spoon. Knives are placed to the right of the service plate with the spoon. Forks are on the left side. Stemware is on the right above the knives and spoon. The bread and butter plate and spreader are on the left side of the service plate. The service plate holds the appetizer, soup and salad courses. The service plate is removed before the dinner plate holding the entrée is served. The napkin may rest on your service plate or be placed to the left of your forks. (See Illustration 1)

An informal place setting is ideal for luncheons and casual meals. If there is a salad fork, it may be placed to the left of the dinner fork when the salad is served before the entrée. Occasionally, the dessert spoon and fork are placed above the plate. (See Illustration 2)

Sitting at round tables of eight or ten people can present some dilemmas in determining which is your bread and butter plate or glass of water. It's helpful to remember that you drink beverages from the right and eat from the left. Your bread and butter plate and salads are on the left side of your plate next to the forks, all beverage glasses will be above the knives and spoons on the right side. If the person on your left uses your bread and butter plate, place your bread on your dinner plate.

1. Formal Place Setting: Soup, fish course, and entreè

1. Service plate
2. Napkin
3. Soup spoon
4. Fish knife
5. Dinner knife
6. Salad knife
7. Fish fork
8. Dinner fork
9. Salad fork
10. Aperitif or sherry glass
11. White wine glass
12. Red wine glass
13. Water goblet
14. Bread and butter plate
15. Spreader

2. Informal Setting

1. Dinner plate
2. Napkin
3. Salad knife
4. Dinner knife
5. Salad fork
6. Dinner fork
7. Water goblet
8. White wine glass
9. Dessert spoon and fork

If you're not sure about which utensil to use, begin from the outside and work inward. For a first course of soup, the spoon will be to your extreme right of your place setting. A salad fork is usually shorter than the dinner fork. If the forks are the same size, then it doesn't matter which fork you use.

Meals should be eaten slowly and in harmony. Usually everyone waits to begin eating until all are served. The hostess will begin by taking the first bite. In the absence of a hostess, the guest of honor may begin.

It is possible to eat gracefully and converse at the same time. If you are pausing to converse, rest your knife and fork on your plate.

To eat soup gracefully, keep the body erect and incline the body slightly forward. Hold the soup spoon so that the thumb rests on top. The spoon is tipped away from you as you fill it rather than toward you. To avoid drips on your blouse or tie; fill the soup spoon no more than three-quarters full and gently brush the bottom of the spoon on the rim of the bowl or cup. Eat the soup from the side of the spoon. As you lift your spoon to your mouth, keep your elbow down and close to the body. If the soup is very hot, gently stir it from the bottom to the top with your spoon. You may sprinkle two or three oyster crackers into the soup.

If you wish, tip the bowl away from you for the last delicious spoonfuls. When you are finished, rest your spoon on the saucer beneath the cup or bowl or in the soup plate if the saucer is too small.

The salad is eaten with a fork. A knife may be used to cut large pieces of cucumber or tomato. If the salad is served with the entrée, the salad plate is placed to the left of your dinner plate. If there are food items in your salad that you prefer not to eat, such as onion, just push them to the side.

Use your knife and fork to cut meat. If the meat is very tender, the fork alone is sufficient. Don't cut up the entire portion of meat before you begin eating it. Cut and eat a small portion at a time. (See Illustration 3)

Hold a fish knife like a pencil. Use it with your fork to filet the fish and to remove bones. The fork alone may be used to eat fish. (See Illustration 4)

3. How to hold the knife and fork.

The American and Continental styles of using utensils are different, and both are correct. In the American style of eating, one holds the fork in the left hand with the forefinger bracing the back of the handle. The knife, in the right hand with the forefinger extending down the handle, gently cut a piece of meat. Then, place the knife at the top of your plate with the sharp edge facing you. Change the fork to the right hand to eat. To rest your fork during the meal, place it tines up on your plate. (See Illustrations 5 and 6)

4. How to hold a fish knife

In the Continental style of eating, keep the fork in the left hand after cutting a small portion of food and, with tines down, transfer food to the mouth. The knife is held in the right hand and may be used to push the food onto the fork. Rest utensils by placing them in an inverted V. (See Illustrations 7 and 8)

5. American style of eating

6. Rest position: American style

7. Continental style of eating

Never rest your silverware on the table while you are still eating. The proper place of the silverware is on the plate.

To indicate that you are finished, place your knife and fork together across the center of your plate. The European custom is to place the knife and fork together with fork tines turned downward. (See Illustration 9)

In more formal dining, it is customary to wait until all have finished their entrée before any plates are removed from the table. After guests have finished their entrees, the host gives the cue that they are finished eating by placing his knife and fork in the finish position. Dessert is served after the table is cleared of dinner or luncheon plates.

Finger bowls, used when food is eaten by hand, are rarely seen today. When using a fingerbowl, fingers are gently dipped into a bowl of tepid water that may contain a slice of lemon or flower petal. The finger bowl rests on a doily and saucer.

The Asian table

It is a compliment to your Asian hosts to use chopsticks, although utensils will be available. There is a difference between Chinese and Japanese chopsticks. Chinese chopsticks have blunt ends, while the Japanese prefer pointed ends. Using chopsticks takes practice. The pointed ends of chopsticks are used for eating. The larger ends of chopsticks are used to remove food from platters. When finished eating, chopsticks are placed together across the top of the dish or bowl or on a chopstick rest. (See Illustration 10)

8. Rest position: Continental style

Glasses
(See Illustration 11)

Stemware should be held by the stem to keep the beverages cool. The brandy snifter is cradled in the palm of the hand. The aperitif glass (pronounced ah-pare-i-teef) holds 2 to 3 ounces of a drink fortified with approximately 15 to 20 percent alcohol. The purpose of an aperitif is to stimulate the appetite before the meal. Aperitifs include sherry, Dubonnet, and Campari.

9. Finished position

Stemware with medium-size bowls is made for drinks low in alcohol such as table wine and sparkling wine. Dessert wine is also served in glasses with smaller bowls. Cordials and liqueurs have high alcohol content; therefore they are served in glasses with tiny bowls.

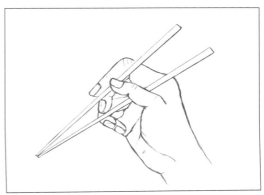

10. Chopsticks

11.

1. Aperitif
2. White wine
3. Red wine
4. Dessert wine
5. Cocktail

6. Champagne flute
7. Champagne coupe
8. Brandy snifter
9. Liqueur
10. Highball

A water goblet (shown in Illustration 1) has a larger bowl than a red wine glass. Use goblets for non-alcoholic beverages such as water and iced tea. Because of their weight, hold them at the base of the bowl.

Before I hire people, I invite them to lunch to see if they are considerate of others.

—Judson Wilson, business woman, author, artist, philanthropist

Refined Points of Dining Etiquette

It is easier to acquire gracious table manners by being aware of our dining habits and customs rather than by what we think is right or wrong. A custom may be correct in one part of the world but not in another. It's customary in some cultures to make a slurping sound when eating soup to show appreciation. In the U.S.A, to make any noise while eating soup is considered rude. In the U.S.A., it is common to eat food with the fork in the right hand. In other parts of the world, people eat with the fork in the left hand with the tines turned down while holding the knife in the right hand. Both ways are correct.

Customs come to us for practical reasons that have been forgotten over time. For example, almost every child is told not to put the elbows on the table. Long ago, the table top was not anchored to a pedestal, and so one was careful not to lean, sit, or put elbows on the table.

We'll show the most graceful and efficient ways to eat and explain how to handle different kinds of food so that you can be relaxed and concentrate on conversation and building rapport with your dinner companions.

Here are some reminders that will enable you to feel and look at ease: Keep hands below your shoulders so that you don't inadvertently scratch your head or run your fingers through your hair. Don't point at someone with your knife or fork or attempt to dislodge something in your mouth with a finger.

Many people have habits of gulping their food and hurrying through their meal. It takes conscious effort to sit at a table and use utensils quietly and gracefully. Habits can be changed. Begin at home, by practicing table manners daily with your family. Whether eating a hamburger, pasta or soup and salad, you'll be more relaxed and enjoy the social interaction as well as the food. And you'll be a role model for your children.

One's social life may also go more smoothly. A budding romance may never blossom if your date is turned off by what he perceives as inappropriate dining habits. And you may never know the reason why you didn't get the second date. Remember, too, that it is just as important to use considerate dining habits when having a meal with your co-workers in the company cafeteria.

Most people wouldn't notice that you picked up the wrong fork or even care. But they will notice a lack of consideration for others. So avoid taking a giant portion at a buffet lest others think there will not be enough to go around, being rude to a server, eating noisily, dominating the conversation, arriving late, and ordering the most expensive item on the menu when you are the guest.

Usually it's a habit of which we are not aware that will pop up unexpectedly. The first ten minutes of our luncheon meeting we are on our best behavior. Then, we begin to relax and perhaps laugh at a comment. That's when we may reach across the table for the salt shaker instead of asking to have it passed.

At the Table

Your posture throughout the meal is important. Sit erect while eating. Adjust your chair at a comfortable distance, and keep both feet on the floor—not crossed. Elbows should not extend more than two or three inches from your sides as you eat or cut your food. Nothing is placed on the table. Caps, books, or purses are placed beneath the chair. Cell phones are turned off or placed in vibration mode, hidden from view. If you have to make a few notes at a business meal, use a small notepad or your palm pilot and say, "Do you mind if I make notes?"

If you are a guest in a private home, pause after sitting down at the table. If the host offers a prayer of thanks, bow your head respectfully.

Napkins

Hosts give the cue that a meal begins by removing the napkin from the table quietly. It is not given a flourishing flip to open it. A luncheon napkin is completely unfolded. A large dinner napkin may remain folded in half, folded edge closest to the body. The napkin is not tucked beneath the chin unless you are eating lobster. The napkin is never used as a handkerchief or to hide food. Use the napkin to blot the lips after taking a bite of food and before drinking from your glass. If you excuse yourself from the table and will return, place your napkin on your chair. When you're finished eating, drape the napkin loosely and place it on the table slightly to the left of your place setting. Use a handkerchief or tissue for an unexpected sniffle or sneeze and turn your head away from the table.

When to begin eating

Begin eating when the host picks up a utensil and takes the first bite. By taking small bites of food, you can easily converse. Don't stab food, but rather pierce it gently or scoop under it. Dispose of something you can't swallow in the least offensive way. (see Pasta Panic and other Food Fears in this chapter)

Rolls and Bread

Break rolls and bread with your fingers. Break off a piece of roll about the size of a walnut, add butter and eat. Slices of bread may be broken into fourths. Hot biscuits are cut with a knife. Butter or jellies are taken from the serving dish to your bread plate or dinner plate before being put on your roll.

You may wish to finish eating a delicious sauce or gravy on your plate by breaking off a piece of roll or bread, placing it onto your plate and, with your fork, gently swishing it around.

Finger Food

Foods that may be eaten with the fingers include crisp bacon, olives, small appetizers and hors d'oeuvres and thin crisp French fries. It is acceptable to use the fingers to pick up small bones to eat inaccessible bits of chops and game birds. Fried chicken and barbeque ribs may be eaten with the fingers on picnics and in family gatherings. However, in a restaurant, use the knife and fork. When you are in doubt about whether to use your fingers to pick up food, follow the lead of your host.

If your sandwich is served open-faced, you may wish to use a knife and fork because it will be cumbersome to eat as a closed sandwich. Pickles and tomatoes falling out of your sandwich do nothing for your professional image. Before you begin eating a sandwich or hamburger, cut it in half. You can continue to make eye-contact with your companion by not hunching over your sandwich as you eat it. Use a knife and fork on chunky French fries in an upscale restaurant.

Problems at the Table

Choking: If you feel like you are choking on something and the first two or three coughs do not provide relief, do not leave the table to go to the restroom. Instead, place your hand around your neck and signal for help. I was at a banquet recently and sat across the table from a woman who began to choke. She held her hand to her throat and started to turn blue, not making a sound. My dinner companion and I could see what was happening and we immediately called out for help. A doctor at a nearby table immediately jumped up, gave her the Heimlich maneuver and she quickly recovered. A doctor was available, which was fortunate. However, everyone should know how to assist someone who is choking.

A *faux pas*: If you should happen to spill a beverage, quickly use your napkin to blot it. If it happens to your dinner companion, offer your napkin. If the unthinkable happens—you accidentally spill wine on your companion—give a simple apology, and offer to pay for the dry cleaning. Or, if you break an antique glass, offer to replace it or pay for it. Other diners at the table should pretend that they didn't notice the accident and continue their conversation.

A little humor helps when you've made a *faux pas*. For example, if you spatter pasta sauce on your white shirt, make a humorous remark such as, "Looks like I now have a red polka dot shirt." Don't dip your napkin into your water glass and try to spot-clean your shirt at the table.

A gracious host will minimize a *faux pas*. Accidents should be attended to with the least amount of distraction and comment. At a cocktail party, a friend wiped up white wine she spilled on a white carpet with a red paper napkin; resulting in a red stain on the carpet. She was embarrassed. She felt worse when the host walked through and said, "Who made this mess?"

Buffet dining

At a buffet, help yourself to whatever you enjoy eating but do not pile food on your plate, and if you go back for a second helping, use a clean plate. As you help yourself from hot foods on a steam table, replace lids to keep the food hot.

Do's—
- Be complimentary.
- Say, please pass…And thank you.
- Take cues from your host.
- Cut and eat one small piece of meat at a time.
- Put sauces and catsup on the side of your plate.
- Pass food counter-clockwise.
- Offer the rolls to your companion before helping yourself.
- Pass salt and pepper shakers together.
- Stir and drink beverages noiselessly.
- Taste food before adding salt.
- Use a toothpick only in private.
- Carry tissues with you in case of a sniffle.
- When finished, leave utensils in finished position.

Don'ts—

- Don't be finicky. If there is food on your plate or in your salad that you don't wish to eat, push it to the side of your plate. Don't pick it out.
- Don't gulp beverages, chew on ice or swirl water in your mouth.
- Don't groom yourself, apply make-up, or comb hair at the table.
- Don't stack dishes when finished.
- Don't play with utensils or wave them as you speak.
- Don't lean back on two chair legs.

Questions:

Q. What should I do when the person sitting next to me uses my bread and butter plate?

A. Forego using a bread and butter plate. Put your bread on the side of your dinner plate.

Q. Is it appropriate to order an alcoholic beverage when you are at a business lunch?

A. Unless you have an established relationship with your companion, do not order alcohol at a business lunch. At an evening business meal, have no more than one drink or order a non-alcoholic beverage such as iced tea, water or juice. Take your cue from the host.

Q. If I drop my knife on the floor, should I pick it up?

A. If you are in a restaurant, you may ask your server to bring you another knife. Pick it up if it falls into the aisle where someone may trip over it. If you are in someone's home, retrieve the knife yourself.

Directions for coughing, sneezing, or moving before the King and Queen

In the first place, you must not cough. If you find a cough tickling in your throat, you must arrest it from making any sound; if you find yourself choking with the forbearance, you must choke—but not cough.
—*Fanny Burney, 18th century writer*

Tip: **You'll feel more confident and in control when you cut and eat small bites of food (and you won't choke).**

CHEERS!

A smile is your best feature.
—Rosemary Schlachter, Consultant
25th Hour

Cocktail Parties and Receptions

Being inclusive, being sensitive to the moment instead of looking for the biggest fish in the crowd, can lead to hidden treasure.

A gentleman suffering from Alzheimer's sat on the couch alone. He and his spouse were guests at a cocktail party at a friend's home. Another guest, noticing him sitting alone, went over and sat down next to him. They conversed for fifteen minutes. This scenario did not go unnoticed by the man's spouse, who later learned that the person who so graciously spoke with her husband had her own interior design firm. A few weeks later, the interior designer was hired to completely redecorate the working spouse's office, city apartment and shortly after to decorate their new home in the suburbs.

Social gatherings such as receptions, cocktail parties, at sports and cultural events are opportunities to connect with others. Once you've accepted an invitation, you go—unless there is a dire emergency. A host who has not heard from his or her invitees can properly call for an answer several days before the event. If your invitation includes a deadline for the response, call on or near that date. Word your inquiry tactfully, such as, "Vince, I hope you received our invitation for the party Saturday night. We were wondering if you are able to join us."

If you must decline the invitation, you do not have to give a reason. A simple, "Thank you for inviting us, we are unable to come on that date" is sufficient.

Make conversation a priority by knowing the purpose of the event. If you are entertaining clients at your local museum's re-opening party after renovation, arrive early. Familiarize yourself with floor plans, the locations of exhibits, food and beverage stations and rest rooms. Request an agenda for the event and a list of guests who have accepted your invitation. An organization's representatives are considered the reception committee to greet clients, help take coats, make introductions, mingle and offer refreshments. Remember that this may be one of those rare times to connect with supervisors, managers, and senior management. Your team spirit image is enhanced when you offer to assist with the party or event by helping with greetings or by handing out name tags.

The times you are with your clients in a relaxed social way are extraordinary opportunities to connect. Your clients may share information with you that will enable you to provide better service to their organizations.

You want people to know you, and there are ways to stand out in a positive manner: Introduce yourself and introduce guests to one another, be complimentary, dress appropriately. Come prepared with a couple of topics of conversation of current news events, books you've read or movies you've seen. Avoid excessive shop talk, gossip and sensitive topics of religion or politics. Answering or making cellular phone calls at a social gathering is unacceptable except in an emergency.

If someone comes up to your group, do not immediately stop talking. If you do, the newcomer will think he has intruded on a private conversation. Welcome the newcomer with a gesture and eye-contact. At the first pause in the conversation, introduce the newcomer.

We all have been in situations where we need to extract ourselves from a conversation in order to greet other guests. You can make a graceful exit after introducing your guest to one or two other people. You can also invite a guest to the buffet table or the beverage station where you will both mingle with others. As your chat winds down, show gratitude by saying, "I've enjoyed talking with you, Roger."

A gracious guest will greet the hosts or those sponsoring the event before heading for the buffet table. When you accept an invitation, you also accept the hospitality of the host. It is inconsiderate to attend a function and say, "I couldn't eat a thing, I just had a big meal." Your host has taken great pride in planning an event that he hopes will please his clients, and that includes food and drink. It can also be a challenge if you are attending two or three social events on the same day and food is served at all of them. Do accept the hospitality, even if it's only one or two tidbits of food.

As a representative of your organization, invite your guests to the buffet table before helping yourself. Since these events usually take place late in the afternoon, it's a good idea to eat beforehand so that you can focus on mingling.

The buffet table will tempt you with delicacies that may be eaten with fingers, forks, or toothpicks and dipped in sauces of chocolate or cheese fondue. You should be able to do all this neatly to avoid dripping chocolate sauce down the gown of another guest, or dribbling wine on your host's white carpet as you attempt to juggle plate and glass. To avoid these *faux pas*, start with just two or three hors d'oeuvres. Do use a plate on which you will place your meatball or chocolate dipped fruit after you have speared it with a toothpick from the chafing dish.

Remember, no double dipping. Once you've taken a bite of celery that has been dipped in sauce, do not dip it a second time. By putting a spoonful of the dip on the side of your own plate, you can dip all you want from your own plate. Don't finger the food. Once your finger has touched an hors d'oeuvre or cookie, it is yours. After helping yourself, move away from the buffet table.

It's hard to avoid the juggling act at parties where seating is non-existent. Since connecting with others is the main purpose, be prepared to eat and drink lightly. If you stand near a table or ledge, you can rest your plate or drink. Carry your drink glass in your left hand so that your handshake is not icy. You can also eat finger food with your left hand so that you can readily give a handshake.

It's our imagination that we think we are brighter or wittier after a couple of drinks. You can drink one alcoholic beverage or none. Alternate with non-alcoholic beverages and eat food. If a guest over-imbibes, call a taxi-cab to take him home.

Arrival and departure times depend on the event. If the event is in a public place, arrive early so you'll have more time to mingle with people. If it is held in a private home, arrive at the appointed time.

If there is an agenda, such as at a grand opening, be early so that you are present for the ribbon cutting ceremony. Most cocktail party invitations, such as a holiday open house, indicate beginning and ending times. People come and go, staying forty-five minutes to an hour; arriving no later than forty-five minutes before the end time. If your company is entertaining clients, you, as a representative, should be early and stay the length of the event to greet and socialize with your clients.

At holiday parties, a guest says farewell by making an exit with the greater part of the crowd. Express appreciation to those who planned the party and to the hosts.

Hostess Gifts:
See The Art of Gift Giving, Chapter 10.

Tip: To avoid the uncomfortable feeling of walking into a roomful of strangers, arrive at the starting time. You will then be greeting other guests as they arrive.

A guest is God's gift.
—*a Persian Saying*

Home Entertaining

The Gracious Host

Many people enjoy entertaining their friends and business associates in their homes. It is a compliment to be invited to a home. The planning for the occasion can be simple or elaborate. Cocktail parties and buffets are usually less expensive and more versatile than sit-down dinners. A dinner party can be formal or informal. Informal gatherings can include birthday parties, brunches, picnics, barbeques, a holiday open house, or a light supper after an evening at the theatre. Weddings, anniversaries, bar mitzvahs usually need to be planned far in advance.

When you entertain at home, you have to plan and organize. Choose a date taking into consideration the availability of your guests. The invitations set the tone of your party. You may choose a theme such as a Halloween party, pool party, or birthday party and coordinate invitations, food and decorations. Invitations may be extended by telephone to get a commitment and followed up with a written invitation.

The number of guests will depend on the type of entertaining and how many will comfortably fit into the spaces of your home. Usually, fewer people are invited for a sit-down dinner than are invited for a cocktail party where people mingle.

A good party does not have to be expensive. Think about the cost of food and beverages plus rentals of chairs and tables if needed. Will you hire a caterer to prepare and serve all or part of the food? Include in your budget, the cost of entertainment, music, flowers and decorations. To hold costs down, limit rentals by supplementing with items you own or can borrow. If you hire a caterer or bartender, provide your own liquor and bar setups.

Have on hand a non-alcoholic alternative for your guests. To avoid someone getting tipsy, offer food with drinks and limit the time of the cocktail hour. Don't let a guest leave your party to drive home who has had too much to drink or eat. Arrange for a ride or put your guest up for the night.

Some last-minute details: Check bathrooms for needed toiletries. Designate a smoking area, put fragile, expensive objects away, have a place for wraps, and ask a friend to take care of your pets or place them where they will not be a nuisance to guests.

The party hosts should mingle, greet and shake hands with guests as they arrive and often a hug is appropriate. One of the loveliest welcome gestures was given by a friend when visiting her home for the first time. She came down the walkway, gave my husband and me each a warm handshake and said simply "Welcome to our home."

In another home, a nine-year-old grandson helped to greet holiday guests at the door with, "Welcome to the Geisselbrecht home."

When you are hosting in your home, young children may be included at the beginning. Older children can help greet, hang wraps and, in other ways, be helpful. It's educational for children to see how Mom and Dad interact with guests. Tell children in advance who is coming.

Since young children are not discriminating, be careful about what you say in front of them.

A host should never leave his guests to attend another event. A friend related an experience she had of attending a party where the host couple was absent. When the guests arrived, they found a note telling them to enjoy themselves. The host couple had gone off to another party, leaving their guests to entertain themselves.

The Welcome Guest

Envision what you would want if you were the host. When you receive an invitation with an RSVP, you respond and indicate whether you will or will not attend (See Invitations, Chapter 14). When you are invited to a home for dinner or a party, arrive at the appointed time. Have the invitation and telephone number with you so that you can call if you are delayed for more than a few minutes by an emergency.

As soon as you arrive, greet the hosts. When you depart, again, seek out the host and make a comment about the delightful time you've had. If it is a large gathering and you can't find the hosts, you may slip out quietly.

If you accept an invitation for cocktails and dinner, then you must stay the entire evening. If you can not stay for dinner, make it perfectly clear that you'll attend for cocktails only. Dinners, whether prepared by the host or catered, are paid for even if they are not eaten.

Never ask to bring an extra guest to a sit-down dinner. If you and your spouse are invited for a sit-down dinner and one is unavailable, explain to the host that your spouse can't attend that evening. In which case, you may be invited to attend alone or the host may wish to include you both another time.

It is appropriate to take a small gift when you are invited to someone's home for a party or dinner. Don't expect your host to open the gift in front of you. You may give a bottle of wine if you know your host enjoys wine; but say that it's for him to enjoy later so that he will not feel obligated to serve it.

Although your host may not ask for assistance, it's courteous to offer; especially if you notice that he could use a little help. A simple "Is there anything I can do?" is sufficient.

A guest contributes to the festivities and shows appreciation for the host's efforts by sending a thank-you note. Among close friends, a telephone call or e-mail note is also appropriate.

If you are privileged to personal or confidential information, keep your lips sealed. At a small dinner party in his home, Jim confided his concern about a sensitive business issue to his guests Ralph and Sue. Two weeks later, the daughter of Ralph and Sue came up to Jim at a supermarket and asked Jim if the issue was resolved. Jim was shocked and disappointed that his friends betrayed a confidence, and he wondered how many other people knew about it.

Q. From which side of the place setting does one serve and pick up plates?

A. Serve plates from the left side of the diner and pick up plates from the right side. You may also serve and pick up on the left. By serving from the left, you avoid accidentally bumping the diner's right arm if he reaches for a beverage.

Q. I have had guests very disappointed that their gift wine was not served. Would it be proper for the donor to call ahead to ask if the guest may bring red or white wine?

A. You may place your host in an awkward position by asking if you can bring the dinner wine. The host may already have pre-selected the wine to be served for a meal. If it is a casual gathering or cocktail party, the host may wish to serve the wine.

Tip: A thank you note to the hosts is always welcome and appreciated.

Pasta Panic and Other Food Fears

Eating foods such as pasta can present challenges, especially a Cincinnati 3-way, which is spaghetti topped with chili and a mound of shredded cheese. Who hasn't at one time or another looked down at a plate and thought, "Hmm, how do I eat this without making a mess?"

First, be careful about your facial expression and body language when encountering food that is beyond your parameters of fried, mashed, or baked potatoes. Be willing to taste a new dish. You may find it delicious.

How, then gracefully to eat the following?

Artichoke: A whole artichoke is eaten by pulling out one leaf at a time, and the small edible portion at the base of each leaf may be dipped in butter or sauce and eaten by pulling the leaf base through your teeth. Place the inedible portion of the leaf on the side of your plate. After you have pulled all the leaves, you will come to the heart of the artichoke. The fuzz covering the choke is inedible. Scrape the fuzz off the choke with your spoon and then cut the choke into small pieces and eat.

Asparagus at a meal is cut with knife and fork. It can be finger food at a picnic or at informal gatherings when sauce has not been added.

Bread slices are broken with the fingers into at least four quarters. A loaf is cut with a knife. After breaking a slice of bread, butter one quarter at a time and eat. Rolls are eaten by breaking off a bite-size piece, holding it next to the bread-and-butter plate and buttering and eating one piece at a time.

Butter is cut from the stick, or a pat of butter is placed on your bread and butter plate or dinner plate. Remove butter from a foil wrapping with your knife, place on your plate, fold the tinfoil and place it on the side of your plate. Whenever taking butter from a common dish that is passed around the table, always use a clean knife.

Caviar: Caviar is served in a crystal bowl on a bed of cracked ice and accompanied with small rounds of toast. Scoop a small amount onto the toast along with garniture (if served) and eat with the fingers.

Cherry tomatoes are eaten whole if they are very small, otherwise, they may be cut very carefully—so that they don't shoot off the plate.

Chops are eaten by cutting off the meat with the knife. Cut the meat from the bone of small lamb chops, and then you may pick up the bone with your fingers to eat the last tasty morsels. Often, chops are served with a paper skirt on the charred end of the bone. Use this to hold the chop to protect fingers from grease.

Raw clams or oysters on the half shell are extracted with a seafood fork, dipped into sauce and eaten in one bite. Informally, at a clam bar or on a picnic, the shell may be picked up with the fingers and the clam or oyster and juice sucked off the shell.

Steamed clams are lifted out of their shell with a seafood fork. The sheath of a steamed clam is slipped off the neck and discarded. Dip the clam into broth or butter and eat it in one bite. Informally, you may use your fingers to remove the clam from the shell. Don't eat a steamed clam that is still tightly closed after being cooked.

Corn on the cob, on casual occasions, is eaten with the hands or with corn cob holders, buttering a few rows at a time. If you are serving it at a more formal meal, cut the cob from the corn before serving to guests.

Crudités (pronounced cru da tay) are cut up vegetables. When served at a meal, they are placed on the bread and butter plate or on your dinner plate.

Danish pastries may be cut into halves or quarters and eaten with the fingers or with a fork if they are very sticky.

Desserts

Cake is eaten with a fork, cutting it with the side of the fork.

Pie is eaten by cutting it with the side of your fork. If it is served with ice cream, such as pie a la mode, it may be eaten with a fork and spoon.

Puddings are eaten with a spoon.

Fish is tender enough to eat with only the fork. If the waiter does not bone your fish, you can bone it yourself by using your knife and fork. Cut the fish and open it so that it lies flat. Slide your knife underneath the backbone and loosen it so that you may lift out the backbone, which you place on the side of your plate. A fish bone is removed from your mouth by gently lowering it onto the fork.

Fondue is a hot dish made with cheese or with meat or fish. Cheese fondue is served in a communal pot. Each guest is given a long-handled fork to spear cubed bread and dip into the cheese sauce. The teeth do not touch the fork tines when eating cheese fondue. Meat fondue or fish fondue is served by spearing the meat on the end of the long-handled fork and dipping into the hot stock. However, a separate dinner fork is then used to eat the meat or fish.

French onion soup is eaten very carefully. The melted cheese on top can be a challenge. Wind some of the melted cheese around your spoon. You can also use the side of your spoon to gently cut the cheese against the edge of your soup cup.

Fried chicken is eaten by using a knife and fork in more formal dining and may be eaten with the fingers at picnics and with family and friends.

Frog legs may be eaten with the fingers or knife and fork.

Fruit

Berries served in a cup are eaten with a spoon.

Stewed fruit is eaten with a spoon.

Cherry seeds are removed from the mouth by lowering them onto your spoon and placing them on the side of your plate.

Fresh whole apples and pears are quartered with a knife and eaten with the fingers. If you wish, you may peel each quarter.

Poached pear: Hold the pear steady with a fork while you spoon the fruit from it.

Cantaloupes are eaten with a spoon when cut into halves or quarters. Use a fork for chunks of cantaloupe. Slices of melon on a plate are cut with the side of the fork.

Grapes are eaten by breaking or cutting a small cluster of grapes from the bunch rather than picking them off one at a time. You may drop seeds into your hand and deposit them on the side of your plate.

Watermelon is cut with the side of the fork, and seeds are removed with the fork. Eat watermelon with the hands only on casual occasions such as picnics.

Hors d'oeuvres (pronounced "or derve") are eaten with the fingers. Hors d'oeuvres are light appetizers served as an extra course or a snack. If plates are offered, take hors d'oeuvres from the serving tray to your plate before eating. If there are no plates, use your paper napkin to hold used toothpicks and remnants from food such as stems and seeds. Never put toothpicks back onto the serving plate.

Lobster: This is one time you're allowed to tuck your napkin into your collar or wear a bib. Twist off the claws and crack each claw with a claw cracker or nut cracker so that you may eat the meat with a pick or shellfish fork. Bend back and twist off the tailpiece, break off flippers and use a shellfish fork to push or pull the meat out of the tail. Cut the tail meat into bite sized pieces and dip into melted butter. You may also break off the small claws to suck the meat out. Crack open the body to eat the red roe and green tamale. The empty shells are placed on a separate bowl or plate.

Mussels: Remove the mussel from its shell with a fork, dip into sauce and eat in one bite. At an informal affair, you may pick up the shell with the mussel in it and suck the mussel off the shell. The sauce may be eaten with a spoon, or you may swish a piece of bread in the sauce with your fork tines.

Nuts are eaten with the fingers. At a table or cocktail party, a nut spoon is provided to spoon nuts from bowl to plate.

Olives, served as a garnish or hors d'oeuvre, are eaten with fingers. Remove the seed from your mouth with fingers and place on the side of your plate.

Pasta: A purist eats spaghetti by taking a strand or two of spaghetti with the fork, bracing the tines on the side of the plate and winding the spaghetti onto the tines. Some people use a spoon to rotate the spaghetti onto the fork. Others find it easier to cut it with the side of the fork.

Pastry (see Danish)

Petits fours are small sponge cakes decorated with fondant icing. Large petits fours are eaten with a fork, small petits fours (of a bite or two) are eaten with the fingers.

Pizza wedges are eaten with the fingers. They may also be eaten with a knife and fork.

Sauces such as catsup are placed on the side of the plate and the food is dipped into it.

Shrimp cocktail is served in small compotes with sauce and eaten with a seafood fork. Dip the shrimp into the sauce and place the whole shrimp into your mouth. Attempting to cut shrimp with a knife or fork is awkward. They may be eaten in several bites. Since the sauce is not shared by others, you can redip the uneaten portion. Shrimp served at a buffet is placed on your plate and sauce spooned onto the side of your plate. If there are no plates, dip the shrimp into the sauce while holding your paper cocktail napkin beneath to catch drips. Fold the inedible tail into your paper napkin—but never put it back on the buffet table.

Snails (escargots—pronounced es car go) are held in one hand with your fingers or small tongs; remove meat with a small fork or pick. You may use pieces of bread on the end of your fork to dip into the buttery sauce.

Shish kebab is cubes of meat and vegetables speared on a skewer and grilled. Remove the food from the skewer by using the tines of a fork to steady the skewer. The skewer is pulled from the meat and vegetables with the other hand.

Sorbet (pronounced sorbay) is a fruit ice that is served between courses to freshen the palate. Since it may just have been removed from the freezer, hold the serving dish at the base as you eat a spoonful or two.

Sushi and sashimi (pronounced su she and sah shem ee) are popular Japanese foods. Sashimi is just seafood. Sushi has rice and other ingredients. Consume in one bite after dipping in soy sauce and wasabi.

Tea: Iced tea is stirred gently if sweetener is added. The teaspoon is placed on the saucer or on a paper napkin if there is neither a saucer nor another plate.

Hot tea: Consider it an honor to be invited to serve tea at a private or public event. Graciously serve guests before serving yourself. Some people take cream or lemon with their hot tea, but not both at the same time. The tea bag should never remain in a teacup while you drink it. Put the teabag into a pot to steep. When removing a teabag, do not try to press out the last dregs with your spoon. A friend confessed that when she tried to press out the teabag, the bag caught on the spoon and flipped onto another woman's white dress. At a tea where guests will be standing and mingling, fill tea cups two-thirds full.

Tip: **If you have food in your mouth that is inedible, such as gristle, remove it inconspicuously onto your fork and put it on the side of your plate.**

Place Cards

Place cards do more than indicate where someone sits. They are keys to connecting with your clients and visitors.

Take time to refresh your memory and familiarize yourself with guests' and visitors' names before your meeting or event. By doing so, you will welcome your guests more warmly. You will convey the message that you have been anticipating their arrival.

There are always protocol issues at official events. Such was the case when The Center for Holocaust and Humanity Education of Hebrew Union College-Jewish Institute of Religion in Cincinnati sponsored "A Day of Recognition." During World War II, leaders of Bulgaria and Denmark were heroic in their efforts of rescue and resistance during the Nazi persecutions. Guests comprised thirty dignitaries from the two countries, including Princess Cheryl and Prince Boris Leiningen of Bulgaria, ambassadors from Bulgaria and Denmark. Religious figures were also among the 350 guests—including Cincinnati's entire political power structure for a full day of festivities and ceremonies.

Two of my friends, Mary Hemmer and Carole Rigaud, were co-chairpersons of the "Day of Recognition." I was asked to be chairperson of the first event, a festive brunch. It was important to become familiar with the names and pronunciation of all the guests, especially dignitaries and those participating in the program. Reviewing the guest list was time well spent. The Metropolitan Club in Covington, Kentucky, with its panoramic view of the Cincinnati skyline, was the perfect venue for the official welcome. As the guests arrived, each was given a place card with a table assignment. Even with the name review, it was difficult to understand many of the guests' names as they introduced themselves. One guest approached the table hesitantly and said his name,

"Michael Bar-Zohar." Immediately I smiled and said, "Dr. Bar-Zohar, you'll be speaking about your book, *Beyond Hitler's Grasp*." Michael smiled from ear to ear to be so recognized as the guest speaker.

Another gentleman approached me in the hallway and said, "Hello, I'm Alfred Gottschalk." I replied, "It's so good to have you with us today, Rabbi."

You see, by reviewing names, you'll know who's who and who should be addressed by professional titles. You'll act and feel more confident meeting and introducing your guests to others by being familiar and practicing aloud the pronunciation of their names.

 At the end the day, Dr. Bar-Zohar commented to Mary Hemmer that the events of the day were executed beautifully. In my mind, it all started with friendly greeters and name recognition at the brunch to make guests feel welcome.

Place cards are always used at formal dinners. The cards are written with the titles. For example: Dr. Claypool, Judge Wilke, Mr. Gore, Mrs. Gore, Ms. Daley. If it is an official event, only the title is used because only one person holds that office, that is, Mr. President, The Vice President, The Ambassador of Belgium. Write only the first names on place cards at informal gatherings of family and friends. Always review place cards to make sure names are spelled correctly.

"The Honorable" is a title held for life when a person holds or has held high office at the federal, state or city level.

Use place cards when there are ten or more guests. Place them above the service plate or on top of the napkin.

Never change a seating assignment by moving your place card except in extreme circumstances—as in the case where someone needs to assist a frail spouse.

If your company is hosting a client event, select people with excellent social skills to staff the reception table. If a guest gives his name and there is not a place card with his name, you may ask if his reservation was made in another name (he may be someone's guest). Do not make an issue over a missing place card or say you don't have a reservation for your client. Instead, say, "Jim, We're so glad you could come. We can seat you at table eight." (Have extra seating available in the event people were inadvertently omitted because of a misplaced reservation). When someone's name has been omitted by mistake, you have to go out of your way to make them feel welcome and do the very best you can to take care of them in a gracious manner.

An omitted reservation happens to all of us at one time or another. My name was not on the reservation list for a dinner meeting. The president of the organization, standing nearby and hearing the conversation, said, "We have space at the head table for Marja."

If it is a large event, it is helpful to your guests to have a floor plan of the tables and their numbers outside the doorway to the banquet hall so that they are not roaming all over the hall looking for Table 42.

As a guest, arrive early so that you are familiar with the seating and can guide your spouse or other guests directly to your table.

In addition to place cards, it is gracious to have a card on each table listing the names of all the guests seated at that table.

Seating Plans

Formal business and social occasions require seating plans. Some informal gatherings may not call for a seating plan. At an informal gathering, take your cue from the host. The host may say, Ellen, you sit here, and Tom will sit next to Judy. Or, the host may simply invite guests to sit where they like. At formal and informal gatherings, men wait for all women to be seated. At formal social events, the man who sits to a woman's left holds her chair.

Formal lunches and dinners require seating plans. At banquets you are given a table assignment (your table number). A table chart is placed outside the banquet room so that guests may locate their tables. Assistants should be stationed around the banquet room to assist guests. Take into consideration people with special needs such as those using wheelchairs.

At a formal dinner, the woman guest of honor is seated at the right of the host. The man guest of honor is seated to the right of the hostess. The second ranking man is seated at the left of the hostess. The second ranking woman is seated to the left of the host. Other guests may also be seated according to rank or position as numbered in the illustration (Men = M, Women = W). In traditional arrangements of 6 or 10, 14 or 18 guests, the host and hostess sit opposite one another. Married couples may be seated by other guests rather than seated together (see illustration 1). If a guest requires additional help, such as cutting food, seat the guest next to his or her spouse or assistant.

At official and formal occasions, guests are seated according to protocol. At other times, make an effort to seat people according to congeniality.

Rectangular or oval table

Man Guest
of Honor

| W | M | W | M | W | [Man Guest of Honor] |
| 2 | 4 | 6 | 5 | 3 | 1 |

Host [ ]   Hostess

| 1 | 3 | 5 | 6 | 4 | 2 |
| [Woman Guest of Honor] | M | W | M | W | M |

Woman Guest
of Honor

Illustration 1

When there are multiples of four, the host and hostess do not sit opposite
one another without having to seat two men or two women together
when there is an equal number of each sex present. If men and women
are to be seated alternately, the hostess moves one seat to the left so that
the man guest of honor sits opposite the host (see illustration 2).

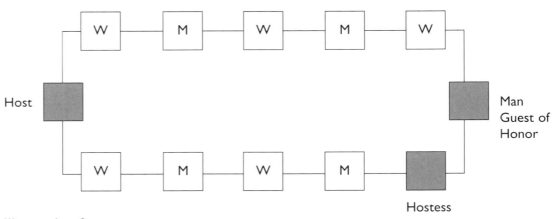

Illustration 2

A single woman may seat her woman guest of honor at one end of the table and herself at the other end. If a man has been invited as acting host, he is seated to the left of the woman guest of honor. The man guest of honor is seated to the right of the hostess. Seat other guests around the table alternating men and women (see illustration 3).

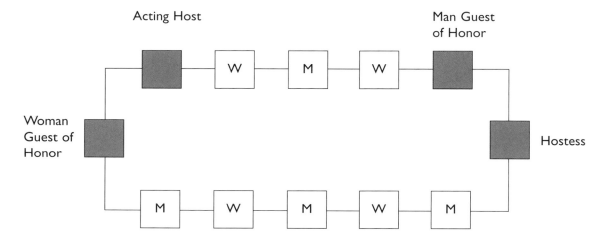

Illustration 3

When a single man entertains, he may invite a woman guest to act as hostess to balance a table when the number is not divided by four (see Illustration 4). When a woman entertains, the seating roles for women and men are exchanged.

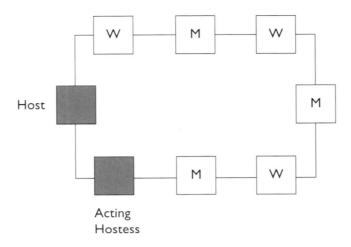

Illustration 4

Many people favor round tables for formal and informal luncheons and dinners. It is more gracious for the host and hostess to sit apart, rather than together (see illustration 5).

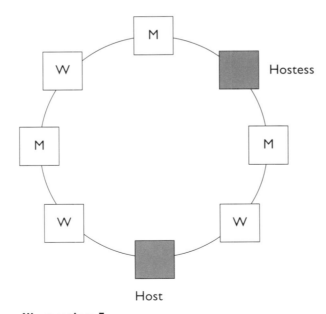

Illustration 5

When a couple requires two tables for guests, at home or in a restaurant, each should host a table. If there are more than two tables, invite a guest at each table to act as host of that table.

Banquet

All seats should be filled at the speakers' table. If an invited guest does not come because of illness or other emergency, another guest should be invited to sit in the unoccupied chair. The host or chairperson sits at the center of the head table, with the guest of honor to his right and the second ranking guest to his left. The emcee, if there is one, sits to the left of the second ranking guest (See illustration 6).

4	2		1	3
Emcee	Second Ranking Guest	Host or Chairperson	Guest of Honor	Spouse of Host

Illustration 6

Table manners include everything from sitting down at the beginning of a meal to leaving the table at the end.

Chapter 12

The Art of Tipping

The meaning of the acronym TIPS originated during the days of Samuel Johnson and the first coffee houses in England. People dropped coins in a box *to insure prompt service*, thus TIPS.

Knowing who to tip, when, how and how much is important to the business person as well as the leisure traveler. An amount may be suggested. However, you may be inclined to be more generous if the service is extraordinary. Tips are not obligatory. Tips are a reward for attentiveness and commendable service.

Rudeness is never acceptable when giving a tip. Treat service personnel the way you want to be treated—with respect. A tip should be given cheerfully and in a generous manner.

There are no exact figures for tipping. The amount of gratuity can depend upon whether you are in an elegant establishment or modest one, a big city or small town, or upon the kind of service you receive. A generous gratuity for excellent service is always acceptable as is less or none for poor service.

One commonly asked question is whether or not to tip for poor service. As a business person, you will feel obliged to tip. However, you may want to adjust the amount. If you usually tip fifteen or twenty percent, consider tipping five percent less when you are displeased. You can make a comment to the maitre d' as you leave about the poor service or call or write the restaurant manager.

The best time to complain about poor service is during the meal. Tell the captain or maitre d' politely that you are dissatisfied and explain why.

When you receive the check, go over it to make sure a gratuity has not automatically been added. In some restaurants a gratuity will be added to the check when there is a group of people.

Restaurants

A guest does not offer to tip or augment the host's tip. A **wait person** is tipped fifteen percent of the bill before taxes are added. If the **captain** mixes the Caesar salad or flames the dessert at your table or provides other special service, designate five percent on the bill. Twenty percent is also appropriate if the service is exceptional or for large parties (check to see if the gratuity has been included in your bill).

The **wine steward or sommelier** who makes recommendations and serves wine is tipped fifteen percent of the wine bill before tax, presented with a thank-you as you leave. Always tip the wine steward in cash, usually after the last bottle of wine has been poured or as you leave.

If you have drinks while waiting for your table, tip the **bartender** fifteen percent of the bar bill before going to your table.

The **bus boy** is not tipped. Usually, members of the wait staff give the bus boy a percentage of their tips.

The **chef** is not given a tip. However, give the chef your compliments.

A **buffet wait staff** is left a ten percent tip; more if special service has been provided.

The **maitre d'** is usually not given a tip. If you frequently patronize a restaurant, tip the maitre d' or hostess five dollars occasionally. At holiday time, give a gift of twenty-five dollars to one hundred dollars.

The host quietly motions to the waiter for the bill toward the end of the meal, at the time coffee is served. Figure the gratuity quickly, rounding it off to the nearest dollar.

The check will have a space where you designate how much to tip the wait person and captain. If your total tip is twenty percent before tax, give the captain five percent and the wait person fifteen percent.

If the bill is presented on a tray, and you pay by credit card, it is signed and replaced face down. If you pay by cash, leave the cash on the tray.   If the bill is presented in a wallet, place your cash or credit card in the wallet and leave it on the table. Your wait person will pick it up and return your credit card or change in the wallet. If you did not include your tip on your credit card, leave a tip in the wallet. Do carry extra bills and change in your pocket for tipping that you do not include on your credit card. If you pay by credit card, carry two cards just in case there is a problem with one of them.

Other employees to remember with tips are:

Cloakroom attendants: One dollar per coat. Tip extra if you have also checked parcels. As the host, keep some bills in your pocket so that you can tip for your guests.

Washroom attendants should receive at least fifty cents and more if a special service is performed.

Room service: In addition to the room service charge, which is automatically added, tip the waiter fifteen percent of the bill and not less than two dollars.

Strolling musicians may be given two to five dollars depending upon how many requests they play. Usually a **piano player** who plays background music has a jar on the piano for tips. Use your discretion in tipping when you make requests. Even if you do not make a request, a nod of appreciation to the musician is always appreciated.

A bellman receives one dollar per bag but no less than three dollars. If there is a lot of luggage, tip five to ten dollars. Tip the bellman at least five dollars for an errand outside the hotel.

The doorman should be given one to three dollars for hailing a cab. In addition, if he assists you with your bags, tip one dollar per bag and not less than two dollars.

A parking attendant should receive one dollar when your car is delivered, or more if the person helps with luggage and packages. If you park your car in a garage, give the attendant who brings the car one dollar or more. Give a generous tip during the holidays.

Valet parker: When the parking attendant brings your car, tip two dollars.

Housekeeper: One dollar per night per person and more if it is a luxury hotel. Leave the tip on the pillow.

Concierge at an elegant hotel: No tip for small services such as recommending a restaurant. Other services such as making your restaurant reservations, tip five dollars. If the concierge obtains theater tickets, limousine service, arranges babysitting or performs other special services, tip ten dollars or more. Place the tip in an envelope and hand it to the concierge with a warm thank-you.

A newspaper delivery person should receive a tip of ten to fifteen dollars at the holidays.

Taxis: Tip fifteen to twenty percent of the cost of the fare for courteous service. If the fare is five dollars, tip at least one dollar. Tip more if the driver assists you with your luggage.

Limousine driver: Tip twenty percent of the bill if a service charge is not included in the bill.

Personal services

Barber or stylist: Tip fifteen to twenty percent of the bill, give one or two dollars to the person who shampoos your hair. A gift at the holidays to your regular stylist is appropriate.

Massage therapist: For a one hour massage ($65 range), tip fifteen to twenty percent.

Tipping in a private club: Ask your host if it is appropriate. Most private clubs do not allow tipping.

Food deliveries: Tip one to five dollars depending on the size of delivery and distance.

Mail Carrier: The U.S. Postal Service asks that gifts given during the holidays have a cash value of no more than twenty dollars. You can also send a letter of appreciation to the supervisor.

When you travel

Customarily, cruise ships have tipping schedules for the service personnel. You are given this information while you are on the cruise. Before you travel, you can contact your travel agent to inquire about who to tip and how much to tip. Generally, allow approximately fifteen percent of the total per person cruise cost for tipping.

Airport skycap: Tip one or two dollars per bag for processing your bags curbside or tip the same amount if they are delivered to the airline counter. Do not tip in-flight personnel.

Lobby attendant: No tip is expected for opening the door or calling a taxi from the stand. Tip one dollar or more for help with luggage or finding a taxi on the street.

Restaurants: In many countries outside the U.S.A., a service charge to cover gratuities is automatically added to your bill.

Respond promptly. Put yourself in the other person's shoes.
You're giving a party, and you hope you've picked a good day.
You want people to come.
—Mark Schlachter

Chapter 13

Invitations

Y ou endear yourself to your friends, clients and co-workers when you participate in their life's most revered ceremonies and celebrations. Consider it an honor that you are invited. You may receive written or verbal invitations to dinner parties, the company holiday open-house, a reception to welcome a customer's new president, weddings, showers, Bar and Bat Mitzvahs, ribbon-cutting ceremonies, retirement and going away parties, golf outings, fund-raisers and meetings of all kinds.

An invited guest assures future invitations and creates good will by responding promptly to an invitation. Respond to an invitation in the manner in which it is given, whether in writing or in person. Express appreciation even if you can't accept it. If the invitation is by word of mouth, accept by saying, "Yes, we'll be happy to attend." You don't have to give a reason to decline an invitation. Write or telephone with a simple, "Thank you for inviting us, but we are unable to attend that evening." If you wish to accept at another time, you may add, "We'd love a rain check."

RSVP printed at the bottom left corner of an invitation is a request for you to call or write to accept or regret. Respond immediately or within a day or two so that the host will know how much food and drink to order. If you lay the invitation aside, you may forget—and find the invitation buried in a stack of papers six months after the event. The inviter has probably been giving you the cold shoulder. Now, you know why.

At the time you accept an invitation, inform your host or event organizers if you are vegetarian, have food allergies, or for religious principles can not eat certain foods. Do not wait until you arrive for the event and then make a fuss. The gracious host will ask about dietary restrictions when an invitation is extended. This is the time to ask about the appropriate attire for the occasion if it has not been included in the invitation, or you are uncertain.

A formal invitation requires a formal response. For example, an invitation to a wedding and reception has a fill-in response card that you return:

Dr. & Mrs. Richard Jackson

will _____*gladly*_____ attend

Number attending _____*2*_____

Some response cards simply have you check mark acceptance or regret and do not include the number attending because so many people misunderstand this to mean they can invite their friends and family members.

If you are single and your invitation indicates that you may bring a guest, include your guest's name on the response card. However, never take an uninvited guest to a sit-down dinner. If you have a cousin or other house guest visiting, you may call the host for permission to bring your guest to an informal gathering such as a cocktail party.

A formal invitation written in the third person requires a written response if there isn't a telephone number or fill-in response card. Your response is easy to write if you send a note written in the third person. If it is a good friend, send a warm personal note. The note may be written and centered on a note card or correspondence card. Wording for the third-person response follows the wording of the invitation.

Mr. and Mrs. Douglas van der Zee
accept with pleasure
the kind invitation of
Mr. and Mrs. John Middleton
for dinner
Saturday, the eighth of February,
at six-thirty o'clock

If you have to regret because of reasons such as another commitment, illness or being out of town, you can include the reason in the response:

Mr.and Mrs. Douglas van der Zee
regret that
owing to a prior engagement
they will be unable to accept
Mr. and Mrs. John Middleton's
kind invitation to dinner
Saturday, the eighth of February,
at six-thirty o'clock

"The Favor of a Reply is Requested by such-and-such a date" is often used in place of *RSVP*.

"Regrets only" means call only if you can't attend, but don't wait until the day of the event. That's too late. The hosts are already planning on your attendance. Responding promptly saves you the anxiety of choosing between engagements should you receive more than one for the same day. Early responses also enable the host to invite others in place of those who decline.

Don't take invitations lightly. Let's say you are invited to your client's reception to welcome their new president. You don't go, and don't call to regret. Your attendance will be noted because your name badge remains unclaimed on the reception table. This lack of respect for your client becomes a black mark against you and your company. Don't wonder why you are not invited to your client's annual golf outing next year, or why you lose the client.

Recently I attended an elegant reception honoring a celebrity. There were at least thirty unclaimed name badges. The food and drink at this affair cost the company at least fifty dollars per person—much food and good will was wasted that evening.

Even in a remote relationship, it's best not to ignore an invitation. Although an invitation does not obligate you to give a gift, it is a thoughtful gesture to acknowledge the occasion with a penned note, congratulatory card or telephone call. If it is a special occasion that you can't attend, such as an anniversary or a client's grand opening, you may wish to send flowers or champagne to help mark the happy event.

Invitations to fund-raisers also require responses for causes you want to support. Rather than tossing out an invitation to which you have little or no interest, look to see who the chairperson is and who is on the committee. If it's a worthy cause in which one of your best friends or customers is involved, you may decide to attend the event or to acknowledge it with a penned note of best wishes for a successful fund-raiser and include a contribution. A note to the event chairpersons congratulating them on the success of an event will be well received.

After accepting an invitation, cancel only in the case of an emergency. Don't cancel an engagement because something more interesting comes along. If you must cancel a business lunch, place the call yourself and reschedule immediately. It's unthinkable to just not show-up. However, no one is perfect. If an engagement is forgotten, call and apologize. You can also send flowers with a note of apology.

Only in extreme circumstances should a meeting be canceled or an invitation rescinded. A company golf outing is not a good reason to cancel a meeting.

In one of my business etiquette lectures, a company vice president asked me whether a meeting date could be changed. The meeting involved four of his customers, who were flying in to meet with his company's local representatives. After the meeting date was set and all agreed to attend, two of the local representatives called to say they could not attend the meeting. The vice president didn't want to inconvenience his customers with a date change because they had already purchased airline tickets. Before I could respond to his question, a staff member asked the vice president, "Did you know the meeting is on the same date as the company golf outing?" The vice-president turned beet red from his hairline to his shirt collar and gruffly said, "Is that the reason they're canceling?" Needless to say, the meeting was held on the original date with all participants present.

An invitation, whether formal, informal, in writing or telephoned contains the following information:

Who:	The hosts of the party	**Rick and Rose Lux**
		Request the pleasure of your company
What:	Purpose of the party	**at a Kentucky Derby Party**
Date:	Include day and date	**on Saturday, May 7**
Time:	Starting and ending time	**3:00 p.m. until 7:00 p.m.**
Location:	Address and map or directions to party A ZIP code allows easy search on a web site such as Map Quest.	**At home 333 Redbird Lane Louisville**
Response:	How to respond, by what date, and to whom	**Your kind response is appreciated by Monday, May 2, to Rose 859-986-5432 Rose@kdp.com**

It is thoughtful to add other information that will make your guests feel comfortable such as proper attire.

Include at the bottom of an invitation to an open house a line indicating whether the location is wheelchair accessible.

You can increase the attendance by mailing invitations three or four weeks before the event. A telephone invitation can be followed-up with a reminder note. If there are key people you want to attend, call them first and check their availability and their acceptances. Follow with a formal invitation. To assure the attendance at large special events, send out "Save the Date" cards prior to sending a formal invitation. A "Save the Date" card is mailed in an envelope two or three months before an event and should be in a similar design to your invitation.

For important events, the envelope should be neatly handwritten rather than labeled or printed on a computer. Hand stamp invitations and, if possible, purchase postage stamps that reflect the occasion or time of year. Do not run them through the company postage meter machine.

An e-mail invitation to a meeting or casual gathering is treated the same way as a written invitation. Reply as soon as you receive it. Otherwise, you might forget. Your immediate response will save someone the task of sending another e-mail or making a telephone call.

When you invite people for cocktails, indicate the beginning and ending times. For breakfast, lunch or dinner, inform them only of the beginning hour.

When you invite someone for a last-minute gathering, avoid saying, "What are you doing tonight?" It puts the other person on the spot. Instead, explain that you are having a few people over for cocktails to meet a new neighbor. The other person can then decide if she can forego other plans (which may have been a quiet evening at home) in order to join you.

Polished social skills require that you be tactful in conversation and that you don't discuss an invitation that you receive in front of others who may not have been invited.

Questions most frequently asked.

Q. **Is it proper to call people who have not responded to invitations?**

A. Yes. You may call to see whether the invitation was received, and whether they will be able to attend.

Q. **Can you skip the wedding ceremony and attend the reception?**

A. Attend the ceremony and reception if you are invited. It is rude not to attend the most sacred part of the event, which is the ceremony.

Q. **If I can't attend, may I send someone in my place?**

A. No. Do not send someone in your place for business or social events without permission of the host.

Q. **What is the proper way to excuse myself if I have to leave a meeting or party early?**

A. Give the reason you must leave at the time you accept the invitation. Otherwise your early departure may be interpreted to suggest that you weren't having a good time or that you had become ill.

Q. **Is it proper to specify "no gifts" on a wedding invitation?**

A. It isn't necessary to specify "no gifts" on an invitation since an invitation is not a request for gifts. However, wording such as, "No gifts, please; your love and friendship are cherished." is acceptable. Some couples, knowing that friends may want to mark the happy occasion, include in the invitation the name and address of a favorite charity as recipient of donations.

Q. **Is it appropriate to ask who else is invited?**

A. No. Exceptions are social or business events hosted by your organization. As your company's representative, you are also considered a host.

Q. **How long does one stay at a holiday open house when the invitation specifies 4:00 p.m. until 7:00 p.m.?**

A. People come and go at an open house. Plan to stay forty-five minutes to an hour, and arrive no later than an hour, before the end time.

Tip: Most people will feel more comfortable about attending your dinner or event if they know others who will be in attendance, mention one or two names of invited guests whom they will know when you telephone your invitation.

Knowing the do's and don'ts when meeting and entertaining international guests makes us look much more "worldly" and "sensitive" and keeps the focus on the important business and social matter at hand.

—Robert W. Lane, President Shepherd Color Company

Chapter 14

Guidelines to International Manners & Customs

Whether you travel abroad or hold meetings with people from diverse cultural backgrounds in the home office, developing a global perspective is imperative. Preparation is the key. Prepare your mind for new experiences. Prepare to step out of your comfort zone of customs and habits where everything is known and easy. Do not make comparisons or be judgmental. Keep an open mind. Native customs will be different. New learning experiences occur when you let go of conventional ideas of what is "right" and "wrong." By emulating differences, you will save time and have a richer experience.

When you travel abroad, read about the history and geography of the host country, the background of the people, common customs and practices, official languages, the economy, government, national leaders and political parties, and religious and ethnic composition. If you are entertaining visitors from abroad, the same preparation is needed.

Avoid scheduling business trips during the host country's holidays. If you are traveling for pleasure, you might wish to include the holidays and festivals.

An understanding and appreciation of others' beliefs can expand your horizon. A learning experience may be as close as a next-door neighbor who has recently come to the U.S. from India, or your local Rotarians may invite you to be part of a group exchange to another country.

In a global economy of expansion and mergers, a local company's employees may suddenly find that their company has become German or Swiss owned.   New managers from a parent company require big adjustments in communications between the local employees and the employees from abroad. The adjustments require flexibility, sensitivity and an awareness and understanding of cultural differences. Diversity training enables employees to work together more harmoniously and to resolve conflicts when they occur.

The success of Procter & Gamble's International Division can be attributed to the many months of cross-cultural training given to their employees and their families before they are sent to work in P & G's offices abroad.

A young man said to me when we were discussing the customs of other countries, "I haven't had experience with the customs of other countries. But I have a good heart, and I think people can feel that in me."

His sincere statement is partially true. However, differences in work or communication styles can create misunderstandings and confusion. Knowing how to acknowledge an error in communication, recover quickly and move ahead is vital to having successful work relationships. (See Chapter 5, diversity)

Becoming familiar with social courtesies, appropriate and inappropriate topics of conversation, and gestures and their meanings is a beginning point. A gesture that is accepted in the U.S.A. may be offensive in another country. Our humor and practical jokes may not be appreciated or understood by someone of another culture. Acceptable attire varies from one country to another, as do dining habits and business practices. Being familiar with religious practices and beliefs of another culture broadens understanding.

When you travel to another country, you are an ambassador of the U.S.A. Being comfortable when you travel means first that you understand your own customs and know what customs we value in the U.S.A. Then you are better able to understand other's values.

For example, in the U.S.A. we value informality and friendliness. Yet, almost anyplace you go in the world you will find that customs are more formal—such as the use of titles when greeting or making introductions. Dress is usually more conservative. Businessmen wear suits and ties, and businesswomen wear conservative suits and dresses, simple jewelry, low heels and minimal make-up. In Arab countries, women visitors should dress modestly. High neck blouses with long sleeves and longer skirts are appropriate.

In conversation, we value directness and openness. Others may value indirectness and saving face. For example, what we consider constructive criticism, humor or compliments may not be accepted in the same

way in another culture. Some cultures consider it rude to say "No," and an answer of "Yes" to a question may simply mean "I hear you." In Bulgaria, "yes" and "no" head gestures are just the opposite from such gestures in the U.S.A.

We value control of time, being prompt for an appointment and quick to close a business negotiation. In another culture, relationship building is more important. In many countries, the expression "Time is money" is not necessarily a belief. Punctuality is highly valued in Germany and Japan. In Spain and Italy, punctuality is not as important. Regardless, business people traveling to another country should maintain their professionalism by being punctual for appointments. If a business executive whom you are meeting is delayed, it can make you late for other appointments scheduled for the same day. It may be necessary to schedule only one meeting per day.

In our workplace, we place value on individualism, independence and competition. Others may place more value upon cooperation and the group's welfare. Many meetings may take place, and many people can be involved in decision making. Promotions may not be based on fairness or equality, but on hierarchy, rank or status. In the U.S.A., we often see change as positive and inevitable; others may seek continuity and tradition.

By exposing yourself to people of other cultures, you will learn more about yourself and your world. If there's an International Visitor's Council in your city, you have the opportunity to meet people from all over the world. Some of my most gratifying moments were with visitors from abroad whom I invited to my home. Yes, I was nervous the first time or two because of wanting to please and to serve food that they would enjoy. I quickly learned that fresh fruit, vegetables and chicken dishes were safe choices. My trepidation about entertaining quickly dissipated.

The international guests were eager to know more about our customs, and they were happy to be invited into a private home to see how we live. We also invited some of our neighbors and friends to join us in entertaining our guests. Visitors included a highly placed official from China who came for dinner. After dinner, we all attended a symphony concert. The minister of culture from Ecuador, who also happened to be a singer, wanted to know if I personally knew Frank Sinatra. From a French woman official, I learned that French schoolchildren respectfully stand when a teacher enters the classroom. There were guests from Japan, India, Nigeria, and South America. I currently host a young woman from Bogotá, Colombia, who is studying environmental engineering at the University of Cincinnati.

As an etiquette consultant, I receive requests for advice regarding sensitive issues. A client called to tell me her eldest son was marrying a Japanese girl. The wedding would be in Japan. There were precise issues regarding the wedding invitation, which was to be printed in English and Japanese. Complicating it further was that my client was divorced, a rarity in Japan at the time. Since the mother reared her son, she thought her name should be listed before the father's name. However, that is not the Japanese tradition. In Japan, the father's name is always placed before the mother's name.

A respectful attitude toward the people, the country and its culture is essential. When you are interacting with visitors from other countries, use polite words generously such as "please" and "thank you." Make it a practice always to stand for introductions. Pay deference to your international guest by making introductions. Give your guest a place of honor at your table either next to you or someone of importance. If you are given a business card, accept it with both hands, look at it, repeat the name to make sure you are pronouncing it correctly, and place it on the table in front of you if you are in a meeting. Don't put it away immediately (see chapter 1, Art of Introductions).

Relationship building takes place at meals in restaurants or private homes. Be familiar with the dining customs of the country you visit and be willing to have new experiences with food preparation. Don't be surprised if food is prepared in a different manner. Be gracious whether you are in a restaurant or private home. If you are in an Asian country, be willing to use chopsticks; but practice before you go.

Know what topics of conversation to avoid, including religion and politics, based on your research of the country. Good topics are sports, especially soccer in many countries, and Olympic achievements of your host country. Use good English; avoid slang and jargon. Speak clearly and enunciate words slowly.

The following is a sampling of countries and their customs. I have given more space to China and Japan because of recent emergence of economic ties between our cultures.

China

"Welcome." These characters can be seen at most international airports, including the Cincinnati/Northern Kentucky International Airport. The greeting can be used on a banner, on napkins, or on the cover sheet of a presentation. It is used at the beginning of an activity or event as well as at its conclusion. The greeting was inscribed with icing in Chinese characters on the rim of the dessert plate at a banquet for ten Chinese delegates from Xi'an. It was held in honor of the Chinese businessmen and women who visited Cincinnati.

Based on ancient Chinese practices, businesses are born out of friendship. It can take months or years to complete business negotiations with the Chinese. Today, in modern China they prefer to make friends with you first before embarking on a business relationship. Therefore, much of the "dancing" or "prelude" to the preliminary discussion and ultimate nego-tiation focuses on whether the friendship is worthy. This "relationship-building" process may mean mutual visits to HQ or branches, factories, and customers, sprinkled with side trips, gifts in kind, or services in kind. To a Westerner, this may seem like an expensive investment toward a goal. However, if you were truly friends, money would be no object. Hence "buying into a friendship" becomes a prerequisite to doing busi-ness with the Peoples Republic of China, with no guarantee of a favorable result—especially in a "buyers" market. In the old days, many Chinese based their business decisions on the stars and their lucky days. Today, this may or may not be practiced.

To understand the Chinese culture, one has to be aware of the following: *Guanxi*, which refers to connections and the related favors owed between you and others. *Guanxi* is based on giving and collecting favors between family members (immediate and extended), friends (most of whom were made during high school or college), and co-workers. Favors granted in the past by one can be called in by the debtor to smooth the way for busi-ness dealing and other situations. It's how things are accomplished. This is also known as the "back door." There is a Chinese saying that "It's bet-ter to owe money than to owe a favor." The reason is because the debtor of a favor never knows when the debt is fulfilled. Also the timing, form, size, or value of payment on the debt is solely defined by the collector.

Face: Saving face and giving face is extremely important. Loss of face is caused by not giving someone proper respect as defined by the circum-stances or the person to whom face is to be saved. In conversation, to openly contradict or criticize someone causes loss of face. Instead, tact-fully talk around the situation. To openly criticize destroys surface har-mony. Maintaining surface harmony is important. It is the art of being polite and courteous and not showing one's true emotions. Giving and saving face is a great way to obligate that person to you for future "collection" in the name of *guanxi*. The value of this act can be invaluable to the beholden one; hence, your *guanxi* with him. If he is an important figure in business or politics, he becomes reciprocally invaluable.

Respect for age and rank: The Chinese have great respect for age and rank. The eldest or highest ranking person in a group should be greeted by you if you are the host or introduced to you if you are the guest. In politics and business, the title supersedes the gender. Use courtesy titles of Mr., Ms., Mrs., and Miss. Madame is used for married women of high rank in business or in politics. The surname precedes the given name and is said after the courtesy title, such as Mr. Lu Yajing. Lu is the family name. In business, one would be introduced to "Factory Director Lu," or "Minister Wang" in politics. Titles are used in conversation, and people address one another in the third person and don't say "You." For example: "How is Mr. Roe?" "Does Mayor Chen wish to have tea?" "Is Office Manager Lee ready for the meeting?" "I really appreciate Mrs. Tu's hospitality." In modern China, men and women are treated equally in public by using job titles or political titles before the family name.

Make introductions with the highest ranking or eldest person's name said first, using the courtesy title of Mr. or Ms. followed by their title. For example:

> **"May I introduce Director Mr. Lu Yajing of the Technology Development?"**

Informally, when a man and woman are introduced, the man is presented to the woman. First say the woman's name:

> **"Ms. Cheng, I would like to introduce to you Mr. Wong."**

Since age is revered in China, a young person may wish to appear older to gain more respect from co-workers. To counteract a youthful look, a man can grow a moustache, but keep it well trimmed. A young woman can appear more mature if she wears make-up, nail polish, wears her hair in an up-do or pulled to the back of the head in a bun.

When introduced, shake hands, and say *"Ni hao,"* (pronounced nee how) and present your business card with both hands. It is polite to accept, with both hands cupped, a business card offered to you. If you go to China on business or you welcome Chinese visitors to your firm in the U.S.A., have bi-lingual *ming pian* (business cards) printed. Current-day simplified Chinese characters (fewer strokes) are read horizontally, left to right. There is a trend among modern Chinese businesspeople to use a classical version of Chinese characters on business cards. Classical Chinese characters are read vertically.

In conversation, refer to China as China or the Peoples Republic of China; not Republic of China. Refrain from saying Red China, Mainland China or Communist China.

How do Westerners refer to the Chinese? Chinese people prefer to be called "Chinese." People of Chinese descent, who live in other countries, also prefer to be called "Chinese." However, if you do not know if they are "Chinese," then it is appropriate to refer to them as Asians first and wait for clarification as the conversation progresses. Do not refer to Chinese people as Orientals or Asiatic—or to Asia as the Far East.

The Chinese speak many tongues and numerous dialects. In an effort to unify the country, people from every province learn Putonghua (people's dialect) which is Mandarin, the Beijing dialect. The country is also unified by the written language. Chinese language contains many homonyms; a simple word may have many different meanings depending on the intonation. However, contextually, it is never misunderstood. And because of this, aural and formal symbols (double entendres) are unique and popular in Chinese culture.

At meals, questions are asked to justify and validate a business relationship. Chinese people often ask personal questions such as "How old are you?" "How much money do you make?" "Are you married?" In addition to personal questions, a Chinese person may say to a friend, "You are fatter than I last saw you…" in a complimentary way. The reference is to financial status—meaning "You're living well" or "You look prosperous." Appropriate topics are local attractions, culture (yours and theirs), life in the U.S.A. and where to shop. Inappropriate topics include sex, government, foreign policy issues and jokes about politics and government leaders, either Chinese or foreign.

The Chinese consider it impolite to say "No." Don't ask directly for a yes or no answer. The Chinese will continue to have meetings with you three, four, or six times until you "catch on." You have to be tuned into the meeting and what is said in order to save time. If you do not get a "Yes" answer or if discussions revert to polite conversation, the answer is "No."

Be aware of customs, habits and gestures. An American will point to his chest to indicate "me." Chinese point to their noses. In China, just as in the U.S.A., pointing at anyone or anything with the index finger is rude. If you must point to something, use an open palm gesture. Respect for personal space is important to the Chinese. Chinese don't hug or kiss in public. However, public hugging between same-sex friends is common. If you are applauded, clap your hands in return. Keep your hands quiet and below your shoulders.

Dress is conservative in darker blue, and gray, beige and brown. Women wear jackets, skirts, long-sleeved blouses with high necklines, pants suits, very low heels and minimal make-up and jewelry. Low-cut or revealing clothes on women are for evening or special occasions. Jeans are commonly worn by men (with a tie) and women (with a nice top) in some business settings. Jeans are ironed and creased. As with our customs, business attire for men is a suit and tie; women wear dressy outfits. Evening gowns and black tie formal dress are worn only at diplomatic receptions.

The gift-giving ritual is part of doing business. A gift to a company, such as a plaque, is not wrapped—so that all may see it. Inexpensive gifts may be presented to a group or organization rather than to an individual. If an individual is given a gift, it should be done privately. Gifts can represent your city or organization and may include a subtle logo. Books, candies, chocolates, and quality writing pens are appropriate. Avoid personal clothing items such as neck ties. A T-shirt with an English slogan is a good gift for a young person or child.   Gift giving can include a banquet.

Homonyms apply to gifts that are aural (how the name of the word of a gift sounds), and formal (symbolic). Numbers contain both aural and formal symbols (based on the phonetic sound, they can have two or more meanings). When giving gifts, the numbers "two," "six," "eight," or "nine" are considered lucky. A gift of "two" doubles the wishes and signifies forever. They can be a pen and pencil set, two boxes of candy or a bouquet of eight or nine flowers. "Nine" and "forever" are homonyms. The names for watches and clocks have the same homonym as the words "death" and "ending." People often give these gifts and ask for a penny to break the spell. This symbolizes a "purchase" of the gift from the recipient, hence not a death wish bestowed upon the receiver.

Colors have significance to the Chinese. Your gift will be well received if it is presented in red wrapping paper. Yellow represents the emperor, and white symbolizes death. Do not use white paper or white ribbon or give anything white, blue or black. The gladiola flower is frequently used in funeral arrangements. Giving and receiving gifts are formal symbols. The Chinese consider it polite to use both hands whether for handling a business card, gift, or a bowl of soup. Do not expect a gift to be opened immediately. If you are given a gift, accept it but do not open it. Open it later.

Gifts, as symbols of friendship, lead to business entertaining at banquets—which include beer (usually served warm), soft drinks, wine or hard liquor, including Maotai made from sorghum and wheat germ that has been fermented. Maotai is used for toasts at banquets and to finalize a business relationship. It is safe to make ambiguous and general toasts. Usually banquets include women, who sit with guests and attend to the guests' needs. The woman may or may not drink alcohol. She is not an "escort" and belongs to the company. Interpreters (male and female) often fill this role.

Chinese banquets can include at least ten dishes (ten is a formal symbol) and they always include fish and chicken (aural symbols). Fish is always the last dish (aural symbol). Diners sit at round tables. At an informal meal, dishes are placed in the middle of the table and people help themselves using chopsticks. Public chopsticks are available for public use. If there aren't any, ask for serving spoons and public chopsticks. Dessert consists of fruit. The tip is included in the bill. In the U.S.A., American customs apply.

France

You will find the French extremely polite and courteous, contrary to the comments you hear about rudeness. The French are proud of their heritage and culture and enjoy good conversation. Meals are leisurely.

Handshakes are lighter and always given when greeting and saying good-bye. Address people with a courtesy title, for example: *"Good day, sir"* or *"Bonjour, monsieur,"* Say, *"Good day, madame"* or *"Bonjour, madame"* to married women and older women. A very young girl is addressed as *"Good day, miss"* or *"Bonjour, mademoiselle"* (although *mademoiselle* is seldom used today). Good friends kiss on both cheeks, men will kiss cheeks of relatives. When French businesspeople present business cards, they state their name, saying the last name first. *Maurice Marto* will introduce himself as *Marto, Maurice.* When leaving, shake hands with everyone and say good-bye and use titles, that is: *"Good-bye, madame"* or *"Au revoir, madame."* Shake hands with everyone, including children.

The French like well-tailored clothing. After all, Paris is a fashion capitol. Men and women should dress in conservative dark colors. Bright or gaudy styles are to be avoided. Business dress in the office is more formal; men wear ties and do not remove their jackets in the offices. Women's jewelry is simple and elegant.

Good topics of conversation include food, art music, books, sports (soccer) and hobbies. You'll want to be informed about the history and politics of France. The French enjoy conversation and like to discuss the politics of other countries. Business can be discussed at meals. Although most business people speak English, do make an effort to speak some common phrases well and apologize for your inability to speak French.

Wine is served at dinner and supper. The host will propose a toast to your health. Eat food with the fork held in the left hand and knife in the right hand throughout the meal except when you wish to rest the utensils and converse. The resting position is an inverted V on your plate. If you are using only the fork, hold it in the right hand. Refrain from cutting your salad with a knife. Break off pieces of bread with your fingers. The French keep both hands on the table (wrists may rest on the table when not eating). To summon waiters call them by *Madame* or *Monsieur*.

Gifts can include books and music. If you're invited to a home for dinner, take candy or flowers. Chrysanthemums should not be given since they are used in funerals. Although it's appropriate to compliment or to thank, a French person may say something like "It was nothing" or "You are too kind."

Many shops and restaurants close during August, which is the favored time for vacations.

Germany

Arrive for your meeting or social gathering punctually. Shake hands with everyone at meetings and small social gatherings when you arrive and when you depart. When you shake hands, give a slight bow or nod and make good eye contact. German people consider it disrespectful to shake hands with one hand in the pocket or to converse with gum in the mouth. Men graciously rise when a woman enters a room.

When introductions are made between two people, say the name of the younger person first. Always use courtesy titles; that is: Mr., Mrs., Ms., Miss. Use the last name in introductions and in conversation until you are invited to use the first name.

> **Mr. =** *Herr (Herr Durr)*
> **Miss =** *Fraulein for women under 20 years of age (Fraulein Durr)*
> **Ms., Mrs., Ms. =** *Frau (Frau Durr)*

Professional people—including doctors, professors, architects, lawyers—are addressed by their profession with a courtesy title: *Frau Doktor, Herr Professor*. When you are introduced to a woman, wait to see if she extends her hand. It is common for German people to greet one another and shake hands each morning even though they have worked together for years. Elder people are deferred to. In business meetings, the eldest person enters first.

After a close relationship develops over a year or more, an invitation to use the first name will be suggested by your German colleague. You'll share a drink and a toast, lock right arms as equals and use the informal form of "You" which is *"Du."*

Good topics of conversation include travel and sports. Soccer is popular. Avoid personal questions such as "Are you married?" or "Do you have children?" Avoid humor at business meetings since business is taken very seriously.

Business attire is conservative. Businessmen wear dark suits, white shirts and conservative ties. The standard business outfit for women is a dark suit and white blouse. Casual business dress includes nice looking pants, shirts, and sweaters.

The largest meal of the day is lunch. Supper, served between 6:30 and 7:30 p.m. is lighter. Business entertaining usually takes place in restaurants. The male guest of honor sits to the left of the hostess, and the woman guest of honor sits to the right of the host. When invited to a dinner party in a private home, bring a small bouquet with an uneven number of flowers (not thirteen), good California wine, fine chocolates such as Godiva or Bourbon Balls. The host toasts everyone and takes the first drink. Eat food, including sandwiches, with the knife held in the right hand throughout the meal and the fork in the left hand (See chapter 11, Eat, Drink and Be Mannerly). Germany is famous for its beers and wines, but public drunkenness is not acceptable.

India

India is the home of many religions. The predominant religion is Hinduism. Approximately 85 percent are Hindu, 13 percent Muslim and 2 percent are Sikhs.

Communications are reserved. The elderly are addressed as "Sir" and "Madame." Use courtesy titles of Mr., Mrs., and Miss when greeting and in conversation. First names may be used after you are well acquainted. Professional titles are used, such as doctor and professor. Greet another by holding your palms together in front of the chin and giving a head nod. Say *"Namaste"* (pronounced nah mah stay) which means "I recognize the divinity within you." When a Western man is introduced, he should shake hands when greeting and departing. Most of the time, Indian women do not shake hands. When introduced to an Indian woman or a man and woman, say *"Namaste."* Indian women hold high positions in education, government and business. Business cards printed in English are appropriate.

A sense of family and belonging is strong. Close friends may be called "uncle" or "aunt." Hospitality is primary because there is no government social security or Medicare; people are dependent on one another. Relationship building comes before any business takes place. Your hosts will ask you personal questions in order to know more about you and your family. They will want to see your family photographs. Reciprocate with similar questions that will show interest in their family. Since Indian people are of a more serious nature, especially on first meeting, refrain from jokes. The people are more casual about time. If someone says that he will call you, it doesn't mean right away.

English is widely used in politics, business and education. Indirect refusals are considered more polite than a harsh "no." If you do not wish to accept an invitation, give a vague "I'll try."

The appearance and dress is modest. Women should avoid revealing clothes, tight jeans and low necklines and wear long pants when exercising. When going into temples, wear long skirts and long-sleeved blouses. Businessmen dress informally in shirt, tie and slacks. Indian women wear saris and other traditional dress. When invited to dinner at a private home (expect to be invited), men wear shirt and slacks and women wear dresses, skirts and blouses or slacks. For formal affairs, men wear suits.

Since Hindus revere the cow because it sustains life, using leather products—including belts and handbags—may be considered offensive, especially in temples.

If you are in a business meeting and are offered tea or sweets, it is courteous to accept the hospitality. Business lunches are frequently held in an office dining room; tables set with linens, china and silverware. Guests in an Indian home may eat food with their hands. Shoes are not worn in the kitchen because it is considered a sacred place. Business women can feel comfortable entertaining an Indian businessman. Hindus do not eat beef and many are vegetarian. Muslims eat beef but not pork or shellfish. Food is eaten and passed with the right hand. It is not appropriate to thank your host for a meal. Instead, say that you enjoyed the gracious hospitality.

When invited to a meal in a home, bring gifts of candy, fruit or flowers. Appropriate flowers are roses, marigolds and jasmine. Don't give alcohol unless you are sure your host drinks. Most Indian women do not drink alcohol or smoke. Wrapped gifts are not opened immediately, but are set aside until the giver leaves.

Italy

Italians shake hands warmly when greeting and departing. A hug and kisses on both cheeks are given only when there is closeness.

You convey the message that you are a successful business person by dressing elegantly. Italy is one of the fashion capitols of the world, where good quality clothing and fine leather accessories are appreciated. For business meetings, men and women wear suits. Men should also wear ties; preferably an Italian silk designer tie. For non-business activities, strive for a chic look with casual dress pants, shirts and skirts. Jeans are fine if they are in excellent condition. People dress up and do not wear shorts in the city. It is considered disrespectful to enter historic and religious places wearing shorts, short skirts, sleeveless shirts or sandals (flip-flops). Men wear dark suits and ties and women wear dresses and heels in the evenings for theater and opera. If you are not sure what to wear for an occasion, ask.

In conversation, introductions and letters, both men and women are addressed by their occupation; always in the masculine form: *Avvocato* Bruni (Lawyer Bruni) (written short version: *Avv.* Bruni), *Dottor* Manzoni (Doctor Manzoni) (written short version: *Dott.* Manzoni). Courtesy titles are:

English	Italian	Pronunciation
Miss	Signorina	See nyor eenah
Mrs.	Signora	See nyor ah
Mr.	Signor	See nyor

Signora (Mrs.) and *Signorina* (Miss) are used only for women when their occupations are unknown.

Defer to the senior or eldest person present when entering a business meeting. You will find that many Italian business people speak English. Business cards are exchanged at business functions, but not at social occasions.

Good topics for conversation include family, Italian culture, music, food, art, wine and films, sports such as soccer and bicycling. Avoid religion, Italian politics and World War II. Italians speak exuberantly and simultaneously with much hand language at business meetings and social gatherings. One must be mindful of how the hand language is interpreted.

Business gifts can include a nice pen or key chain. Gifts to take when you are invited to someone's home are wrapped chocolates, pastries and flowers. Chrysanthemums are not appropriate since they are associated with funerals in Italy.

In a restaurant, first courses include minestrone (soup), pasta or risotto (rice). A second course could include beef, chicken, pork, veal or fish with vegetables. Salad is usually fresh vegetables after the meat. Antipasto (appetizer) may also be served before the first course. Pizza is usually served as a sole meal. The meal ends with dessert, fruit and coffee. Coffee can be ordered in different ways: Espresso (strong coffee), espresso *"lungo"* (little bit lighter), *"ristretto"* (super strong coffee), *"corretto"* (with some liquor) and *"macchiato"* (with some milk). In almost all formal restaurants *"cuberto"* (cover) has to be paid in addition to the tip. The tip is always voluntary, and it will never be shown on the check. *Cuberto* includes the use of napkins, tablecloth, bread and silverware. More informal restaurants don't charge a cover. Restaurants do not usually open for the evening meal until 7:00 o'clock.

In addition to the dinner knife, fork and soup spoon, the place setting may include a fruit knife and fork set above the plate. You may wish to join your dinner companions in eating in the European style of holding the fork in the left hand, tines turned down, and the knife in the right hand. The knife is used to push the food onto the fork. Spaghetti is properly eaten by winding two or three strands onto your fork as it is braced on the side of your plate. At the end of the meal, place your utensils parallel on the plate with fork tines turned down.

*He who smiles rather than rages
is always stronger.*
—Japanese proverb

Japan

The Japanese make introductions by saying the family name first and using a courtesy title: For example: *Yamaguchi Kazuo* is addressed as *Mr. Yamaguchi*. *Yamaguchi* is the family name and Kazuo is his first name. When in Japan, use the person's last name and *"san"* after it. *"San"* is the equivalent of Mr., Mrs., Ms.; for example: *Yamaguchi san*. Only people who have grown up together call one another by first names. Do not ask a Japanese person to call you by your first name in Japan. He will feel uncomfortable doing so. Expect a formal bow when you are introduced, the greater the respect, the lower the bow. When bowing, palms of the hands are held in front of the body facing thighs. A bow and a handshake are appropriate between a Japanese person and a Westerner at the beginning and end of a meeting. It's best to take your cue from the Japanese business person. Even in very informal greetings, there is a slight bow or nod of the head when meeting. Everyone stands for introductions. Whereas we place strong emphasis on eye contact, the Japanese make very little eye contact when greeting or in conversation so as not to make the other person feel uncomfortable. The proper response to an introduction is *"Hagemamashte dozo yorushiku."* (It's my first time to have the pleasure to meet you, please feel kindly disposed towards me).

Because the Japanese live on densely populated islands, space is valued. When you shake hands, allow approximately three feet of distance between you. It is never appropriate to touch in any way other than to shake hands. Public displays of affection are frowned upon.

Meishi, the exchange of business cards, is a ceremony in itself. At the beginning of a meeting, everyone exchanges business cards. It's important to remember they are presented after the bow. The cards are placed on the table in front of you so that you don't have to try to remember everyone's name and position. The card is presented with both hands so that print is easily read by the recipient. The recipient accepts the card in both cupped hands. A non-Japanese business person will have business cards printed on both sides; one side printed in English and the reverse side in Japanese. A business card includes the individual's name, company, address and title. When presenting a card, present it with the English side up. When accepting a card, hold it in your hands and look at it. Do not put the card in your pocket or a billfold as this would be considered disrespectful. Carry a card case for cards you give and receive. Neither should you deface the card by writing on it. The Japanese consider it very important to keep a file of business cards. If you visit or call a Japanese business person with whom you have exchanged cards, you will be treated graciously.

Dress according to your status or position. A conservative appearance in your attire conveys the message that you take the business relationship seriously. Men wear a suit and tie and women wear a suit or dress in conservative colors. Skirt lengths should be knee length or lower. For formal affairs in Japan, men wear dark suits, women wear stylish dresses.

Sitting on the *tatami* mats in Japanese restaurants can be a challenge. Women first kneel and then sit back on the calves of their legs. If this becomes uncomfortable, move the legs to the side but keep them close to the body. So as not to offend, don't sit cross-legged or with the legs stretched out. Men may sit cross-legged on *tatami* mats. At business meetings when sitting in standard chairs, men and women should keep both feet on the floor.

Relationship building can take place at lunch or dinner and is a prerequisite before business discussions. Meal time is when you appreciate and enjoy the food and the beautiful dishes; a time for your Japanese host to get to know you, your age, the university you attended and your company. Demonstrate graciousness by praising their firm and showing appreciation for the opportunity to do business with them. Good topics of conversation are your ideas about Japan, food, sports, your travels in other countries, questions you have about Japan. And avoid discussions of comparisons of your country with Japan and reference to World War II. Colloquialisms can be misunderstood and jokes can backfire. Loud speaking and a confrontational manner is not the Japanese way of doing business.

Be careful with compliments. Compliments are indirect and often shrugged off by the Japanese people. A friend, in Japan on business, complimented a beautiful painting hanging in the office of his Japanese host. The Japanese host wanted to give it to him as a gift. An indirect compliment such as a remark on the good taste of the decor of his office would be more acceptable. Questions that we deem inappropriate to ask are acceptable in Japanese conversation. You may be asked personal questions such as, "How old are you?" In Japan, age is revered. The older you are, the more respect you receive.

The Japanese word *"Hai"*(pronounced Hi) does not always mean yes. The Japanese find it difficult to say no. To say "No,"or *"Iie"* (pronounced ee yeh) is considered rude and does not give the appearance of harmony. And they don't like to disappoint. My brother, Henry, a Rotarian, was hosting Japanese visitors at his vacation home. At breakfast, he asked them if they would like to water ski. He was delighted when they both smiled and said "Yes." At the lake, the Japanese visitors were mortified when Henry encouraged them to put on the skis. The "yes" indicates that your questions are heard or understood rather than met with agreement.

Gestures and body movement are restrained. Keep the hands quiet during conversation, and never point at anyone or anything.

It is an honor to be invited to a Japanese home in Japan or in the U.S.A. It is the custom to remove your shoes when you enter the home. Usually, you will be given slippers to wear.

Table manners are gracious and elegant. Chopsticks *(hashi)* are used to pick up the bite-size morsels of food. When you are finished, place chopsticks across the top of the bowl. Never leave them standing in a bowl of rice as this signifies that someone has died. Soup begins and accompanies the whole meal. An eating custom that is acceptable in Japan is to show appreciation when eating noodles or soup by making a slurping noise. Beer or sake is served before the meal. If you do not wish to drink, just say "None for me" and place your hand over the cup. The correct way to drink a beverage is to use two hands; one hand around the container and the other hand placed beneath it. Always allow someone else to pour a drink for you. You can reciprocate by pouring a drink for your companion.

Napkins are not used. Instead, you are given a hot towel in a basket before the meal. Wipe your hands, but not your face and neck, and replace it in the basket.

You can be more comfortable using chopsticks by practicing at home and in Asian restaurants. Whenever you go to an Asian restaurant, request a pair of chopsticks. I was a guest of six Japanese clients at a Japanese restaurant near the Toyota offices in Northern Kentucky. We all sat on *tatami* mats at a low table. Since we were in the U.S.A., there was the optional knife, fork and spoon at my place setting. I asked the waiter for chopsticks. My dining companions smiled and were surprised and pleased that I would join them in using chopsticks.

All meals include rice, which is considered the staple of life in Asian countries just as wheat is the staple of life in the West. A meal is not complete until you partake of the staple of life with your companions. When you dine with your Japanese friends, you will be served rice. Don't ask for bread. Before you begin eating, say *"Ita daki masu,"* (pronounced ee tah dah kee mas) "Now I partake with gratitude." After eating, say *"Gochiso sama,"* (pronounced go chee so sah maw). "It has been a feast." *"Kekko desu,"* (pronounced Keh co dehs) "I've had enough."

The Japanese people do most of their entertaining in restaurants or bars after business hours rather than in their homes. At karaoke bars everyone is expected to participate in the singing. If the entertaining is at a "hostess bar," businesswomen should not attend. When you entertain your Japanese guests, you will feel more comfortable and your Japanese guests will prefer that you take them to a Western style restaurant. If you entertain in the U.S.A., your Japanese guests might wish some Japanese food after they have been here for a week or two. In Japan, tipping is not customary.

Initial business gifts are inexpensive so as not to incur obligation. It is the gift that counts, not the cost. The most welcome gifts represent your area such as a coffee table book or locally made candy or chocolates, fruit, alcohol such as brandy, excellent wines. Gifts for children can include dolls or theme T-shirts with English words. Gifts are wrapped, omitting ribbon. They are given and received at the end of a visit. And they are presented and received with both hands. Don't expect a gift to be opened right away. If the host insists that you open a gift, do so gently to show appreciation of the wrapping of the gift. The Japanese keep gift wrap, often rewrapping the gift.

Avoid giving gifts of an odd number since they are associated with bad luck. Do not give four of anything because "four" sounds like the word for death in Japanese. Flowers that the Japanese associate with death are lilies, camellias or lotus. If you give white and yellow chrysanthemums, be sure to include other colors such as pink since white and yellow chrysanthemums are used at funerals. Several years ago, I gave a tea for a group of Japanese women. It was fall, and knowing that the chrysanthemum is the Japanese national flower, chrysanthemums seemed appropriate as a centerpiece at the tea table. My guests complimented the flowers and also the hand-painted Japanese vase that had been a gift from an aunt.

Good times to give gifts: *Oseibo* refers to the end of the year time to give gifts for business and to show appreciation to special friends. *Ochugen* is midsummer gift giving time, but not as significant as *Oseibo*.

Relationships will go more smoothly if you learn phrases in Japanese such as for greetings, "Hello" is Kon'ichiwa (pronounced Kon nee chee wah).

Some practical Japanese phrases are:

English	Japanese	Pronunciation
Good Morning	Ohayo gozaimasu	O-hah-yo go zye-mahs
Good Evening	Kon'banwa	Kon-bahn wah
Good Night	Oyasuminasai	Oya suminah say
Thank you	Arigato (Gozaimasu)	Ah ree gah toh
Please	Dozo	dough zoe

Latin America

Latin America includes Central and South America, important trading partners with the U.S.A. There are similarities in habits and customs in the Latin American culture. The official language is Spanish except for Brazil, where the people speak Portuguese. Time is more relaxed. Good friends may confirm a meeting time by asking if the meeting is *la hora inglesa* (English hour) indicating promptness, or *la hora espanol* (Latin hour) indicating arrival of thirty to sixty minutes later than the specified time. One of the reasons that punctuality is more relaxed is because of the emphasis on personal obligations.

Communications are warm and friendly. Standing conversations occur at a closer physical distance than you may be used to. It is considered unfriendly to step back. There are affectionate gestures of touching the shoulders or holding the arm of another. Among friends there is a warm *abrazo* (embrace), back-slapping, followed by a handshake. The *abrazo* is a sign of good will. The greeting is the traditional handshake; a man will wait for the woman to extend her hand. People are addressed by titles. Titles are included on business cards. Refrain from calling people by their first names until you are invited to do so. It is not necessary to include the last name when addressing someone with a title. For example: *Doctor* refers to a physician or Ph.D., *Profesor* is a teacher, *Ingeniero* is an engineer, *Arquitecto* is an architect, *Abogado* is a lawyer. People without titles are addressed as Mr., Mrs., Miss (*Senor, Senora, Senorita*) plus the surname.

Mexico is more "U.S. Americanized" since NAFTA. The three major cities are Mexico City, Guadalajara, and Monterrey, which is close to Texas.

In conversation, refer to the U.S.A. as "North America" rather than America. Instead of American, say "U.S. American." Latin Americans also see themselves as being American. Topics of conversation include the culture and history and art of the country. In Mexico, do not refer to the Mexican-American War, poverty, illegal aliens. or earthquakes. Since, bullfighting is popular, you may alienate your business associate if you make negative comments about it. In Colombia, avoid the topics of drug traffic, politics, and religion. Mexicans will use the "psst-psst" sound to attract another's attention in public. *Manana* doesn't necessarily mean tomorrow. It could mean in the near future or substitute for "no." It is not considered rude. The OK gesture with thumb and finger is considered vulgar.

Be aware that words written or printed in red ink will have a negative impact. In Mexico, Korea and parts of China, the names of the deceased are written in red ink.

Business cards are bi-lingual; English on one side and Spanish on the reverse. Hispanics usually have two surnames. The first one listed on the business card is the father and the second name is the mother. Use the father's surname when speaking to someone. Women often use their husband's surname with or without their own, by adding the preposition *"de": Maria de Gonzalez, Marcela Rodriguez de Castano.* In Brazil, surnames in Portuguese are reversed. The father's name follows the mother's name.

Business dress is conservative—dark suit and tie for men, with white or light blue shirts. Women wear classic style dresses, skirts, blouses, and suits. Casual clothing for men includes pants and light shirts. Women wear blouses, pants or skirts. Avoid jeans and tight revealing clothing.

In Mexico and other Latin American countries, it is necessary to have an intermediary who is known to the business person you are meeting. There are several ways to find an intermediary. Industry trade shows in the U.S.A. and in the country where you want to do business are good sources. You can also form a business partnership with another company that has a non-competitive product and has a presence in the country where you want to do business. The regional export division of your local U.S. Department of Commerce can be helpful and will know of people and companies in your area who can serve as intermediaries.

Business entertaining usually takes place at lunch, which is the main meal. The initial meetings are to establish friendly relationships before getting down to business and may include meeting family members. Breakfast meetings are also popular. When a woman invites a businessman for a meal, she should include other associates or spouses. Although a Spanish man will want to graciously pay the bill, you can pre-arrange to have the meal added to your hotel bill. Know that women of Colombia and Chile have advanced in professions in spite of social restrictions and the machismo ethic. The traditional toast is *Salud*.

Drink bottled water and—wash fresh fruit and brush your teeth with bottled water—but don't make jokes about Montezuma's revenge. When in doubt about food, order it baked or fried.

Business gifts can be small items with a subtle logo. Gifts for the home may be flowers and candy. Handicrafts from home are also appreciated.

Daily Greetings

Morning greeting	"Buenos dias"	Good morning
Afternoon greeting	"Buenas tardes"	Good afternoon
Any time greeting	"Hola"	Hello
	"Como esta?"	How are you?

Poland

Greet people by shaking hands unless you are a close friend or relative, in which case you will kiss on both cheeks. Polish men commonly kiss the hand of a woman when greeting and departing. However, American men will shake hands with women. It is appropriate for a man to wait until the woman extends her hand. Professional titles such as Professor and Doctor are used along with Mr. or Mrs. For example: *Panie Doktorze* (Mrs. Doctor), *Pan Professor* (Mr. Professor). First names are not used unless initiated by a Polish person. The use of first names is accompanied by the formal ritual called *bruderschaft* in which friends share a drink and kiss.

Dress is more formal for everyday life. Shorts are not worn in public except by children. Men wear suits and ties for business, women wear dresses and pants suits. Casual dress includes nice-looking jeans and pants. When invited to someone's home for a meal, men wear jackets and ties and women wear dresses, skirts or dressy pants outfits. Dressy attire is also worn to expensive restaurants.

Traditional social courtesies of deference toward women are observed. They include allowing the woman to go first, men opening car doors and holding the chair in a restaurant.

Conversation includes European politics, Poland and its history, movies, exhibitions, music and art. Avoid discussion of religion and personal questions such as "Are you married?" or "Do you have children?"

The business day begins at 8:00 a.m. after a light breakfast; a second breakfast is taken around 11:00 a.m. The main meal along with tea is eaten after work between 3:00 and 6:00 p.m. A light supper of sandwich or salad may be eaten at 8:00 or 9:00 p.m. Business entertaining may take place at the main meal. The guest of honor is seated at the head of the table. Toasting is made with vodka. A toast is returned by saying, "To your health," The vodka glass may be filled many times; so if you do not wish to drink much, sip and do not empty your glass.

Appropriate business gifts are whisky, cognac, coffee table books, art books and travel books. When you are a guest in someone's home, bring an unwrapped gift of flowers, plus a wrapped gift of candy, liquor, wine or books. Gifts for children such as books, toys or sweets are appreciated.

Saudi Arabia

Greetings: Wait for your counterpart to initiate the greeting. Men shake hands with other men and sometimes women. A business woman should wait for a man to offer a hand. If a woman extends her hand and the Arab man does not wish to shake hands with her, he may pat his chest over his heart to indicate that he accepts her greeting. Follow your host in greetings. The more traditional greeting for men is to shake hands by grasping each other's right hand, placing the left arm on the other's shoulders and exchanging kisses on each cheek. Never kiss or hug the woman. A customary greeting is *Salaam alaykum* (Peace be with you). Then follow with *Kaif halak (How are you?)* after shaking hands. It is customary for Arab men and women who are friends to walk hand in hand.

Despite the heat, men and women should dress modestly in public. For business, men wear jacket and ties, long pants, long-sleeved shirt, buttoned collar, and no jewelry. Women should cover most of the body; never show bare shoulders, bare midriff or wear shorts in public. Women should wear high necklines, full length sleeves, and loose fitting skirts with ankle-length hemlines. A scarf or *abaya* (light weight cloak) will frequently come in handy, especially when entering a Mosque. Also, shoes are often removed when entering a mosque. You can follow the lead of your host.

Conversation about women or asking about a man's wife or daughter is inappropriate since the men are protective of women. A general question, such as, "How is your family?" is acceptable. In business conversation, the person who asks the most questions is not usually the decision maker. The decision-maker is more likely to be a silent observer. When there are moments of silence, don't feel like you have to talk. Communications take much time and include the social niceties before discussing business. Your Arab hosts want to know you as a person. In business discussions, "Yes" might mean "maybe" or, "probably not." Saudis stand close with intense eye contact during conversation. Be careful that you do not back away, as it could offend.

There are hand gestures and body language to avoid: The "thumbs up" sign is considered offensive. The left hand is used for hygiene, therefore avoid gestures with the left hand and don't eat or pass food with the left hand. It is also distasteful to show the soles of your feet. Do not cross your legs. Sit with both feet on the floor.

In the Muslim world, Friday is a day of congregational prayer. Devout Muslims say prayers five times a day. Business meetings do not prevent the saying of prayers, and a Saudi host may excuse himself from a meeting to say prayers. The Muslim religion forbids drinking alcohol and eating pork or pork products; some Muslims do not eat shellfish.

If you give a gift, it will be opened in private. Avoid giving gifts of alcohol, pigskin products, knives, toy dogs, or gifts that picture dogs because the dog is considered unclean. Never give sculptures or paintings or any images of partially clad women. Be discreet about complimenting or praising your host's possessions. The host will feel obligated to give it to you. It is considered impolite to refuse a gift.

Since alcohol is forbidden, fruit juice may be served for toasts. Food should not be cooked in alcohol even though the alcohol is burnt off in the cooking process.

Spain

The Spanish lifestyle has an unusual work day structure. In the main centers of commerce, the attitudes of the long siestas have been revised. Many business people begin their work day at 9:00 a.m., leave their work from 2:00 until 4:00 p.m. to be with their families and return to work until 8:00 or 9:00 p.m. Restaurants usually do not open for evening meals until 9:00 p.m. Punctuality at business appointments and social occasions is not a priority for the Spanish. However, to be on the safe side, it is still important that you be punctual for business meetings.

Men and women shake hands when being introduced and shake hands when departing. Friends, both men and women, may hug one another—and women will also kiss the cheek of a friend or relative.

A Spanish last name includes the surname followed by the mother's maiden name. Mr. *Carrerra Rodriguez*. *Rodriguez* is the mother's maiden name. In conversation, address him as Mr. *Carrerra*. Both names are included in correspondence. Address elders by Mr. or Mrs. and the last name as a sign of respect. However, they may call you by your first name. Business cards are printed in English with Spanish on the reverse. Present your business card with the Spanish side facing your Spanish colleague.

Dining together is considered essential to establishing business relationships. Meeting for coffee, lunch, *tapas* or dinner is vital to successful negotiations. However, it is a time for establishing personal relationships; not for discussing financial matters. If any business is discussed, it is at the end of the meal when coffee is served. A late evening meal can go on into the wee hours of the morning.

An initial business meeting is more social, and business matters are not discussed. This is the time to get to know one another as individuals. You will be asked questions about your background, education and interests. Good topics of conversation include life in the U.S., politics, and sports. After you are well acquainted, discussion about religion, personal questions about family, hobbies or occupation are acceptable. Avoid negative comments about bullfighting. Spaniards are proud of their bullfights. Interruptions in conversation are not considered rude; but are to be interpreted as interest. A gesture that is considered vulgar is the "OK" sign with thumb and index finger.

Women's rights are not as advanced compared with many other European countries. Spanish men will usually accept a lunch or dinner invitation from a businesswoman; however, she must maintain a professional demeanor at all times. If a woman returns a man's gaze, socially or in business, it sends a message of personal interest.

Clothes are conservative for business meetings and business-related activities such as an invitation to dinner. Men wear jackets and ties, and women should wear dresses or blouses and skirts for a more feminine look. The Spanish appreciate an elegant, understated appearance. Short shorts are worn only at resorts and not in public. When you enter places of worship, wear clothing that covers the shoulders.

Gifts of pastries or chocolates are welcome. If you are invited to a home for dinner, take flowers with an odd number of blossoms—that is not thirteen. Do not give dahlias and chrysanthemums as they are associated with funerals, and red roses are for lovers. Gifts are opened immediately. On entering a shop, greet the owner with *"Buenos dias"* (good day) or *"Buenas tardes"* (good evening). When you leave, say *"Adios"* (good-bye) or *"Buenas noches"* (good night).

A toast is given by the host or hostess by raising the glass and saying *salud*. Guests do the same in response. It is the custom to eat with the knife held in the right hand and the fork in the left hand throughout the meal. When you are finished, place your knife and fork side by side on the plate. It is assumed that you are not finished or that you want more to eat if you leave utensils crossed or at opposite sides of your plate.

United Kingdom

England is one of four distinct regions of the United Kingdom, which also includes Scotland, Wales and Northern Ireland. The Scots, Welsh and Irish are not English and are offended when referred to as such. Additionally, they do not consider themselves European.

The English value privacy and personal space. When greeting, men and women shake hands and say, "How do you do." Men wait for the woman to extend her hand. In conversation, maintain a little wider space and avoid strong eye contact. First names may be used in business and socially after a short acquaintance. (Take your cue from the English.) If a man has been knighted, he is addressed as *"Sir"*—*"Sir John."* The envelope is addressed as *"Sir John Tippey."* The Queen is referred to as *"Her Majesty"* for the first time and thereafter as *"ma'am."* If you are meeting royalty, members of the nobility or upper clergy, check polite forms of address in *Debrett's New Guide to Etiquette and Modern Manners*. Refer to a Scot as a Scot or Scotsman, *not* a Scotch (scotch is a beverage). Refrain from jokes about kilts.

Business dress is conservative for men and women and includes dark suits of blue, gray and black. Men's shirts should not have pockets—or, if they have pockets, they should not be used. Wear a solid or patterned tie. Do not wear a striped tie. A striped tie refers to the school or university that one attended. People know the social standing of a person by the tie. For example, a school tie representing Eaton, Campbell or Belfast, indicates that the wearer is a member of the upper middle class or aristocracy.

In the evening, women wear dresses. An evening dinner is not casual. A dress with a décolleté neckline and mid to long sleeves (not sleeveless) or dressy pants are suitable.

In conversation, avoid asking personal questions or criticizing the Royal Family. Good topics are the city, history, architecture and literature. Gardening is a favorite topic. Avoid conversations about money or religion—and in England avoid discussion of Northern Ireland. There are differences in the Queen's English and American English. For example: The English word for drug store is *chemist*; to call someone on the phone is to *ring up* and an elevator is a *lift* and when you go to a doctor's office, it's called the *surgery*.

Doing business requires patience as decisions are not made quickly. Business lunches are held in pubs (short for "public house"). The English pub is a long-established institution. Pubs are filled at lunch time with business people. Numerous drinks that used to be consumed have been reduced to one or two beers. Power breakfasts are only beginning to catch on in England. Business dinners in restaurants are also popular and may include spouses. In Scotland, home entertaining is common. You can reciprocate with a dinner in a restaurant. The months of June, July and August are vacation months and not a good time for business appointments.

Gifts are not part of doing business. However, a house gift such as flowers or quality candy is appropriate when you are invited to someone's home.

In England, toasts are made to the Queen at the end of a formal dinner.

Northern Ireland

Because of the political situation, there is a great bit of difference between Northern Ireland and Southern Ireland. Southern Ireland has become quite wealthy since joining the Common Market.

People greet with hand shakes; a man waits for the woman to extend her hand. Use occupational titles of Dr. and Professor when addressing professional people. Avoid using first names on initial meetings; take your cue from your Irish associate. If your introductions take place in England or the U.S.A., it's helpful to specify whether the person you are introducing is from Southern Ireland or Northern Ireland.

Businessmen are appropriately dressed wearing suits, ties, or tweed sports jacket. Women wear suits, wool blazers, wool skirts in conservative colors. A raincoat is a necessity.

Formal dinners start at 8:30 p.m., and people usually arrive twenty or thirty minutes later. In the British Isles, functions and dinner parties can go on quite late. Don't expect hors d'oeuvres before dinner. At the end of the meal, a large platter of fruit, cheese and figs is passed; at the same time after-dinner drinks are served. Discussions can last until midnight. It's considered a brilliant dinner party when the guests don't leave until 1:00 a.m.   In any event, don't rush away after dinner. One should stay an hour or two. Drinks are not usually served with ice, and so you need to ask for it. You may be given only one or two cubes. The national drink is Guiness Stout served cool.

At a formal dinner party, the host will propose a toast to the hostess. In Northern Ireland and England, a toast to the Queen is made at the end of a formal dinner.

Business gift giving is not a concern. Bring gifts of wine, flowers and quality chocolates when you are invited to a home for a meal.

Conversation topics include the beautiful Irish countryside, Irish handi-crafts, and soccer. Avoid discussion of Northern Ireland's relationship with the United Kingdom, religion and comparisons of Ireland and the U.S.A.

The Knowledgeable International Traveler

When you travel to any country, keep in mind that many international business clients' initial opinion of you begins with their view of the U.S.A. The source of this information can come from web sites, the international studies departments of local colleges and universities, and the embassy of the country you will visit. Whether or not you agree with international perceptions, by understanding how others regard you first, you can better adjust your international business strategies to take into account these perceptions. Be prepared to discuss U.S. policies in a diplomatic manner.

Travel Tips

Don't assume, be judgmental, or compare other countries to your own. Avoid wearing clothes with American designer labels and logos, American flag pins and other U.S.A. symbols.

International business travelers should avoid ostentatious signs of wealth such as wearing expensive gold watches and jewelry, especially in developing countries. Carry a brief case only when needed. Ask permission before taking photos; avoid taking photos of Middle Eastern women. Remain sober, mind your own business and respect the local customs. Leave your opinions back in the U.S.A.

Do make copies of all important documents, including passport, credit card numbers and phone numbers. Carry these separately from where you carry the originals. In case of loss or theft, you can order replacements.

Resources

On Line Resources: International Business Etiquette

- E.Tu Associates: www.etutrade.com
- GLOBALCINCINNATI.ORG
- Governments on the World Wide Web: www.gksoft.com/govt/en
- International Business Etiquette and Manners:
  www.cyborlink.com/besite/
- International Visitor's Council:
  www.Ivccinti.org/getinvolved/indivinvolv.htm
- Japan America Society: www.cincinnatijas.com
- www.Rotaryinternational.org

Note: These web sites were operational at the time of printing.

Books

- Axtell, Roger E. *Do's and Taboos Around the World*. Wiley, 1993
- Dresser, Norine. *Multicultural Manners*. Wiley, 1996
- Esty, Griffin, Hirsch. *Workplace Diversity, A Manager's Guide to Solving Problems and Turning Diversity into a Competitive Advantage*, 1995
- Maggio, Rosalie. *How to Say It*. Prentice Hall Press, 2001
- McCaffree, Mary Jane, Richard M. Sand. *Esquire, Protocol, 25th Anniversary Edition: The Complete Handbook of Diplomatic, Official and Social Usage*
- Sinclair, Kevin with Iris Wong Po-yee. *Culture Shock! China*. Graphic Art Center Publishing Company, 2002
- Visser, Margaret, *The Rituals of Dinner*. New York: Grove Weidenfeld, 1991
- von Drachenfels, Suzanne. *The Art of the Table*. Simon & Schuster, 2000
- Williams, Jeremy, "Don't they know it's Friday." Gulf Business Books, 1998

Other

- CEO Resources: www.ceo-resources.com/team.htm
- Marja Wade Barrett Business Manners Training Seminars
  Marja Wade Barrett Executive Etiquette Seminars
  E-mail: mbarrett@one.net
  Web site: www.marjabarrett.com

Gifts

- www.Greatergood.com
- Freedom Trees: www.freedomtrees.com

Marja Barrett is an author, national speaker, trainer, and consultant on etiquette and social skills to top businesses. She has been honored by numerous organizations including the YWCA, Administrative Management Association, the Internal Revenue Service, Central Region Federal Women's Program, The House of Representatives, Commonwealth of Kentucky, City of Cincinnati, and the Cincinnati Enquirer as a Woman of the Year recipient.

Marja started her business in 1985 after a successful career in the fashion field as a professional model and managing director of the Kathleen Wellman School of Fashion and Modeling in Cincinnati. In-house clients include Fortune 500 corporations, health care and financial institutions, federal government agencies, schools, the hospitality industry, colleges and universities.

Thousands have benefited from her business seminars, classroom sessions, guest presentations, nationally syndicated newspaper articles, radio broadcasts and television appearances.

Marja is a member of Rotary International, serves on the board of the Cincinnati Scholarship Foundation and is a member of the Cincinnati International Visitor's Council as well as a consultant to the Japan America Society. She is a past president of the Northern Kentucky Heritage League and served on the board of the Kentucky Symphony Orchestra. For seven years, she served on the Vestry of Christ Church Cathedral.

Polished social skills give working professionals the knowledge to act with confidence in every business situation—confidence that leads to greater personal success and increased corporate profitability.

Marja Wade Barrett Associates

We custom design seminars to fit your company needs. Participants describe Marja's sessions as entertaining, informative, confidence building and comfortable. We offer programs that can be structured and combined for a two-hour session, a half-day, a full-day, or an evening seminar.

- **Business Manners**
- **Executive Etiquette**
- **Effective Client Entertaining**
- **Dining Skills**
- **Self-Presentation Skills**
- **Communication Skills**
- **International Business Manners and Customs**

Please feel free to call (859) 341-8944
or e-mail us for more information at: mbarrett@one.net
Web site: www.marjabarrett.com

Marja Barrett Associates is available for:
- **Corporate Programs**
- **Private Consultations**
- **Conventions and Association Meetings**
- **Training for the hospitality industry**

Marja Barrett Associates
2165 Tantallon Drive
Fort Mitchell, Kentucky 41017-2084

Business Manners for Success

Marja Wade Barrett

Second Edition

- Connect with clients and customers
- Increase your upward mobility
- Entertain clients with ease
- Improve dining skills
- Develop a global perspective

For Additional Copies of Business Manners For Success
Use the form below

Reply to: Business Manners For Success
             2165 Tantallon Drive
             Ft. Mitchell KY 41017-2084

Please send me _____ copies of **Business Manners for Success**

My check for _____ is enclosed.
(Please make check payable to: *MWB Enterprises*)

1 - 9 copies:	$26.95 + $1.89 tax (State of Kentucky) + $4.00 S&H = **$32.84 each**
10 - 50 copies:	$24.25 + $1.70 tax (State of Kentucky) + $3.00 S&H = **$28.95 each**
50+ copies:	call 859-341-8944

Name _____

Address _____

City _____ Sate _____ Zip _____

Phone _____

Email _____

Thank you!